Paint the Town Red

A Peckham Novel
Book 3

James Court

Paint the Town Red - Third Edition

This novel is a work of fiction. Names, characters and locations are the subject of the author's imagination and any resemblance to actual persons, living or dead, locations or objects, existing or existed is purely coincidental.

It is sold subject to the condition that it shall not by way of trade or otherwise, be lent, resold, hired out, or otherwise circulated without the author's prior consent, electronically or in any form of binding or cover other than the form in which it is published and without a similar condition including this condition being imposed on the subsequent purchaser. Replication or distribution of any part is strictly prohibited without the written permission of the copyright holder.

Copyright © James Court – May 2016

All rights reserved.

ISBN: 1533112231

ISBN-13: 978-1533112231

DEDICATION

To my son Mark

CONTENTS

1. The Only Constant is Change...1
2. Team Tactics...12
3. The Best Laid Plans of Women...24
4. A New Lease of Life..30
5. A Flexible New Approach..34
6. Industrial Cohesion...41
7. High Finance, Low Tactics...48
8. Good Employee Relations...54
9. Old Chickens Come Home..61
10. Never a Dull moment..69
11. Love is in the Air..77
12. Improper Property..86
13. Curiosity..92
14. Negotiation...104
15. New Tricks, Old Dogs..111
16. Yuletide Preparations...117
17. Seasonal Celebration..122
18. Christmas Comes Early...131
19. Goodwill to All Men...137
20. A New Beginning..140
21. Business Bounces Back...150
22. The Sweet Smell of Success...162
23. The Pungent Smell of Disorder..167
24. Painting the Town Red..172
25. Pitfalls in the Course of Love..180
26. Geriatric Gestation..189
27. Life – Peckham Style...196
28. Loose Ends...203

ACKNOWLEDGMENTS

This book was created with the support and encouragement of the members of the INCA project

1. THE ONLY CONSTANT IS CHANGE

Tracey Mulligan sat back and rubbed her eyes. Her long golden lashes quivered as she sat staring at the papers in front of her. She had been going over the accounts and sales projections for the past hour, and there was just one conclusion she could draw. They would be broke within a year. She had taken over the day-to-day running of Hardcastle's French Polish factory, with high hopes of turning it round from a loss making money pit into a profitable business, but although the factory was now a much happier, and more productive, place to work, there was no escaping the fact that the demand for their product was reducing. Britain was shaking off its post-war blues, and entering a brighter, more carefree era. Dark polished furniture had no place in this world of flared orange cord trousers and flower patterned shirts.

She ran her hands along the edge of her brass bound mahogany desk, and looked out of the window at the haze of boiling shellac that indicated that the daily bottling run was about to begin. Everything appeared fine, and the factory ran almost like clockwork. However, there was no disguising the fact that month on month sales were lower than a year ago. The previous management had only realised this fact when the storeman complained about running out of shelf space, and asked if they could use an empty room for the excess.

The then manager, Ponsonby, had attempted to tackle this problem by hiring additional sales staff, to canvas potential customers. The action was a disaster. Ever with an eye to scrimp on costs, Ponsonby had employed the cheapest, and most incompetent, people he could find. Only one of his six new employees ever achieved sales worth much more than his salary, and even his efforts were of little value when you included the cost of long distance telephone calls, and delivery charges to his native Ireland.

It was ironic how the production staff had gone out of their way to please her, and in doing so only made more of the product which they now found harder and harder to sell.

Somehow the job Tracey had always dreamed of doing wasn't as much fun as she thought it would be. Sure, the banter with the managers, and making decisions which others carried out, was every bit as satisfying as she had hoped: but the uncertainty of their long term future weighed heavier on her each day, as she got to know the staff whose livelihood depended on her.

She reached for her modern looking BT Trimphone, and held it steady with one hand, while with the other she dialled her finance manager's extension. Then she sat back, and listened as his own receiver warbled a few doors away down the corridor.

"Henry, can you spare me a few minutes?"

"Give me two minutes to sign these cheques; then I'll come along."

She sighed. Signing cheques meant money going out. What they needed was money coming in. Henry Fothergill had been delighted when she had contacted him to offer him the job that Ponsonby had sacked him from three months previously: well, as delighted as a cold emotionless fish like Henry could be. She had given him a free hand to manage the accounts, a degree of freedom that Ponsonby and Hardcastle had denied him, and he had responded with energy and skill. She was grateful for the way he had sorted out so many of the problems that the previous management had left them with.

Henry Fothergill was not an imaginative man. He could quickly find the last missing halfpenny in a ten-year set of accounts, but would spend an hour deciding between a blue or red tie. In fact, his wife Jane managed his wardrobe, and dictated what he wore each day. It was the only way to get him out of the house, and to work on time. He could, however, always be relied on.

There was a knock at her door, and it opened slowly as if the visitor did not wish to intrude, even though he had been summoned.

"Ah, Henry. Come on in."

Fothergill approached, and sat on the chair in front of her desk. There was another chair at the side of the desk, but that would have implied a less formal relationship, and Henry was not one to impose.

Tracey looked at him, and frowned.

"We're in trouble, Henry. You've done a wonderful job of tightening up on credit control and cutting waste, but the truth is that we are in a reducing market. Half the factory has been empty since Hardcastle took over, other than for the increasing stocks of polish that have filled a few vacant rooms, and the bank will not let us keep deferring repayment of loans for ever."

She grinned at him, but the grin was really directed at the thought of the local bank manager, Mr Wilson, who was ever eager to please her, and whom she regularly pleased in return. She wondered how long passionate nights could stave off mounting interest charges.

"Have you any ideas?"

The question was rhetorical. She did not really expect him to supply the answer to her problem. Once she had finished speaking she immediately regretted putting him on the spot like that. The qualities that made him an excellent accountant were the exact opposite to those needed to answer her question.

"We need another product. Something that is in demand."

It was a blindingly obvious statement, but at least it was a start. She smiled encouragingly at him, the sort of smile that his wife, Jane, would not have approved of. Having met Tracey, Jane had been most unhappy when Henry had been offered his old job back. It was only the absence of other employment offers that stopped her from forbidding him to accept. Jane had first met Tracey when she turned up unannounced one Saturday, seeking information about the factory, in order to prepare a take-over plan. Jane had taken an immediate dislike to the voluptuous tactile blonde who kept touching her husband on the arm and hand, to emphasise points, as she spoke.

Tracey's second visit, once she had secured control of the factory, did nothing to improve Jane's opinion of her, despite the offer of a job which Tracey made to Henry while she was there!

"But what?" she asked, surprised that he had answered so promptly.

"Well, if we are to trade on our product name it needs to be allied to the current range, and if we are to make it worthwhile then it must either fill a niche, or else be made cheaper than our competitors."

Tracey was impressed. She suppressed the urge to kiss him. She had found her outgoing impetuosity misinterpreted by so many of the factory workers, who were not used to such spontaneous expressions of excitement or approval. She smiled again, knowing that Henry was one of the few men in this world who would not be undesirably aroused by her sensual facial expression.

"Who would be the best person to speak to? I mean, who would have an idea worth pursuing?"

This second set of questions was beyond Henry's mental scope. He had thought about the need for a second product for five months, ever since he became aware of the state of the company, but with no success.

"Perhaps if you ask at the monthly foremen and charge-hands meeting?" Henry suggested tentatively, but he knew that the meeting was a somewhat barren desert, devoid of innovation and unlikely to father ideas.

As Henry got up, having exhausted his input into the topic, he hesitated.

"There's one small change we could make, but I'm not sure it would go down very well."

He hovered, reluctant to go, and even more reluctant to say what was on his mind.

"Come on, Henry. You can say what you like to me. I won't be offended."

"It's not that. It's the workforce that I think would get upset."

"Well?"

She patiently waited while Henry decided the best way to say what he wanted to.

"We could get rid of those sales staff that Ponsonby took on. They've scarcely earned us a penny, and they add nine point four percent to the wages bill."

"Ah! But you think that perhaps the rest of the workers would not like the idea of them being sacked? Can we use them elsewhere in the factory?"

"You'd have to ask Tom Dawes, but I doubt it. One of them is allergic to polish, and from what I've seen of them all except two are allergic to hard work. I thought three of them were working quite hard until I realised that they were taking it in turns to keep phoning the same companies trying to cold sell different grades of polish."

"Well, at least they were trying."

"Trying, be damned! One of the companies made ball bearings and another was a chip shop in the Old Kent Road."

Tracey sighed. "So somehow we need to persuade them to leave of their own accord."

Henry gave her a brief, wicked smile: so brief she nearly missed it.

"You have something else in mind?"

"Well, if we sacked one, then the others might go on strike. That way we would save some wages money until the dispute was resolved."

Tracey was amazed at Fothergill's deviousness. It was not a quality that she ever dreamed he possessed.

"Do you have one in mind?"

"Yes. The girl, Jenny. She's had three days' compassionate leave in the past four months. All to bury grandparents."

"That's a bit harsh, Henry. Perhaps the poor girl has been unlucky recently. Sounds like she needs sympathy rather than sacking."

"All grandmothers? And I heard one of the others take a message from her grandmother yesterday. Just how many grandmothers can one girl have?"

"I see what you mean. Let me bring it up at the meeting this afternoon. Perhaps Dawes can use one or two of them elsewhere."

Henry nodded and left. Tracey pondered her options. She had to either get the wages bill down, or else increase sales. And neither was going to be easy.

Held on the first Tuesday of the month the foremen and chargehands' meeting had been convened twice previously since Tracey had taken over management of the factory. At the first meeting the attendees had arrived in their usual paint splattered overalls and torn warehouse coats. At the second a certain sartorial elegance crept in, with a smattering of new work clothes and well brushed hair: those who had hair. At today's third meeting, they had excelled themselves with several examples of Burton suits, flowery shirts and flared canvas trousers.

Tracey sighed. 'If only they had paid as much attention to their minds as their clothes,' she thought.

General production issues were discussed before tea, but they were few. Since her arrival, and daily walks round the factory chatting to the staff, problems seemed to have melted away. The ones that were raised today were quickly met by voices eager to please the boss, by offering solutions. The speed with which solutions were proposed, made Tracey wonder if the issues were manufactured in order to impress her with pre-created answers.

During the tea break there was an absence of the usual noisy slurping, and many a little finger stuck out daintily as they bravely swallowed the canteen assistant, Edith's, evil brew without adverse comment. No one was quite sure just why Edith's tea was so foul, but it was consistently so, without fail.

After tea, Tracey outlined the problem of falling sales, and asked for ideas for new products. There was little response. The factory staff were used to being told what to do, not provide management with ideas. If they had been a football team or a record then they would have been labelled the 'B' side. The brightest of the staff had left with a previous management team, when the factory was sold to Hardcastle. Of those remaining, many would have considered the Luddites too progressive.

In fact, most of them were shocked at the very thought of assisting management in this way. Tracey was not convinced that some even understood that the factory going bust would mean they would not have jobs.

One young foreman raised his hand tentatively, as if in school, and waited to be invited to speak.

"Yes, Darren?"

"Could we make paint, Miss?"

A dozen heads turned to glare at the spotty youth. Darren was the loading bay supervisor. A role he got by default, as the only person left on the bay when Hardcastle bought the factory. Most of the long-term foremen looked upon him as a glorified errand boy, and had little respect for him.

"My Dad has just decorated the scullery. He used distemper, and it rubs off on you as you walk past. He says that emulsion paint is too expensive."

Tracey let her eyes roam along the ranks of the production foremen.

"Don't look at me! I've no idea how to make emulsion paint. Besides, you're talking quantity, not quality. Our equipment just isn't set up for it."

It was the Millwall team foreman who spoke. A man who struggled to stop his crew talking long enough to start work on a Monday: particularly after a home defeat on the Saturday. Tracey let her gaze run along the row of faces, who now all sought to avoid her, whereas five minutes ago they each wished to catch her eye.

But Darren had not yet finished.

"Lots of people are painting walls, instead of papering these days, even lounges and dining rooms."

The foremen immediately returned their attention, and faces, towards Darren: grateful for an excuse to avoid eye contact with Tracey. The faces of many of the older men showed their displeasure at his temerity in speaking in front of his betters, and using words like *lounge,* instead of the traditional *parlour,* which they had grown up with. In their collective minds there was nothing wrong with painted room walls, as long as you were talking about the outside lavvy, and whitewash was the product of choice for that. Clearly this was a young man did not know his place, and was hell bent on causing trouble.

"Thank you, Darren." said Tracey, as she gave him one of her knee weakening smiles. "That could be just the sort of product we should investigate. I guess, however, that we would have to look outside for help in setting up a production line."

Darren blushed: a blush that started on the cheeks, and slowly spread to the tips of his ears. The other men scowled. Not only was the boss praising the upstart, but now she was talking about bringing in outsiders. Well, it was not unexpected; after all she was an outsider herself.

At this point, old entrenched attitudes finally gained the upper hand, and stifled the novelty of having a very attractive and friendly woman boss. She was simply another member of the management class, exploiting the workers for the sake of money. In an instant they reverted from eager to please, to non-thinking mode. A mode where initiative is looked on as a character defect, and change is despised, as an attempt to interrupt the balance of the daily 'us and them' conflict called industrial relations.

The meeting ended with little further discussion, and each scurried back to their waiting staff, who had no doubt taken advantage of their absence to slacken the pace of work.

Tracey had decided that the meeting was unlikely to be helpful, or even sympathetic, to her problem with the useless sales staff. She would speak to the general foreman, Tom Dawes, privately about the matter. Although watching his expressionless face during the meeting did not give her cause to be hopeful. As the men filed out of the room, she remembered something else she wanted to discuss with the storeman, Harry Derry.

"Mr Derry, could you spare me a few minutes, please?"

Harry paused, and turned as he heard his name spoken. He had been daydreaming of events many years ago. He did that a lot recently, especially when she was about. The new boss wore the same perfume as his late wife, and just the smell brought back vivid memories which he thought the years had taken from him.

"Miss Mulligan?"

"Come and sit here with me," she said, indicating a chair in the front row next to where she now sat. "And please, Harry, call me Tracey."

Harry smiled wryly. She was not unlike his Lizzy in some ways, and in age much like he supposed a daughter would have been, if Mother Nature had not played such a cruel game with them. He approached, *Evening in Paris* getting ever stronger with each step.

"Now, Harry! If we did go into paint production, how would that affect storage?"

Harry thought for a moment.

"Large tubs? Like our bulk polish cans, or bigger? This building is hardly made for that. We'd need stronger shelving, and handling them all day would soon wear out young Reg. One of those electric fork-lift trucks would be nice."

Tracey nodded. Reg Swinton was the junior storeman. Tracey had used all her charms and powers of persuasion to get him the job a year ago, when she was trying to track down a former managing director of the company. Reg was recently released from prison at the time, and she made great use of his criminal skills in the first few months that he was employed there. She was unsure of how much Harry knew about his activities, or of her involvement.

"Yes, your assistant is a bit puny. But we have plenty of space if we were to make suitable alterations. Have a think about how we could go about it. I'll speak to you again in a few days."

Harry nodded. He was having difficulty concentrating, with the perfume so strong in his nostrils. But the prospect of another one to one chat with her was something to look forward to. He attempted to make intelligent conversation to hasten such a meeting.

"I'll look into it, Miss. I mean Tracey. It's mainly a matter of floor strength and door widths. And..."

He hesitated.

"And what, Harry?"

"Well, the factory is laid out all wrong. The production and storage should be in the basement and ground floor, with the canteen and offices above."

"Yes. I agree, but that would take money and time to organise. If we don't make a profit soon then we won't have either."

She placed her hand on his arm as she continued. "I'm sure you will do your best Harry. I look on you as one of the most sensible members of staff."

Harry grinned. Being compared to some of the production teams was not a high compliment, but at least it was a compliment. Ccoming from her, even a rebuke would have been welcome attention. Hardcastle and Ponsonby had only ever grunted or grumbled on the rare occasions when they had spoken to him. Besides, since his wife died he had spent little time in female company, especially company as curvy and delightful as Tracey. He decided he should make a move to get back to work, before he said something foolish.

Reluctantly he rose, took a slow, deep, breath in through his nose, and made his way to the stores. As he sat at his desk he savoured the lingering scent of perfume in his nostrils, although he could not be sure if it was really still there, and not a memory of his late wife.

"Anything interesting, Harry?" asked Reg as he watched his dreamy eyed boss sit and stare out of the window.

"Well, apart from us going bust if we don't find something else to make, and the boss asking me to work out how we could handle bulk liquids, no nothing at all, Reg."

Reg Swinton watched Harry as he spoke. He had that same faraway look in his eye that he always had on the rare occasions that he spoke of his late wife.

"That same perfume again?"

Harry nodded.

"I think I'll go and get a mug of tea before I check the stock."

Reg glanced up at the clock and frowned. The canteen closed an hour ago, but Harry seemed to have lost all track of time. The whistle would blow in five minutes and they would join the rush to clock out.

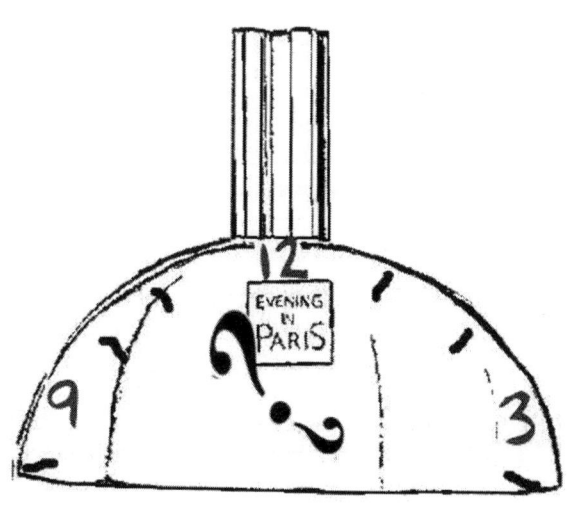

2. TEAM TACTICS

Tracey found Tom Dawes in the Crystal Palace supporting production workshop. She beckoned him away from the noisy claret and blue bedecked room, out into the corridor.

Dawes listened carefully to her summary of the problem with the sales staff. Then he shook his head.

"No use to me," he said. "One of them took a week to work out his route from the front door to his office. He kept ending up in the Millwall workshop. Don't know what he thought the blue and white painted door meant. Besides, from what you said earlier we need to shed production staff, not increase them."

Tracey nodded. He was right, but she was clutching at straws, and really wanted his opinion on another angle: Henry Fothergill's suggestion.

"What do you think would be the reaction of the production staff if we were to sack them?"

Tom shook his head again. It was not a question he expected her to ask him. She was the proprietor, and he was a worker. Nowhere in his job description did he remember seeing anything about advising management about economics, or staffing matters outside of the production teams.

"Not sure the men would like that."

"Even if it was in order to preserve jobs elsewhere?"

Dawes smiled. Suddenly he remembered the way Stanley Capes's had handled getting rid of an objectionable union representative some years ago.

"Perhaps if we could make them unpopular with the workers first, and then sack them. But it would need careful handling. Leave it with me for a few days."

Tom Dawes was not an imaginative man, but given an example he was capable of copying it. Two years ago, before the company had divided into two, the general foreman had been a man called Stanley Capes. Stanley had set in motion a rumour about an unpopular union representative, which had resulted in the workers agreeing wholeheartedly when the man was sacked. But the man was almost universally disliked to start with. Capes's ploy had mainly been to justify their action to the union, and to thwart the possibility of external union picketing, rather than placate the staff. But it might work.

The workers Tracey was referring to were neither liked nor disliked. They were widely considered an economic waste of space: the product of the recruitment policy of the previous management, which looked more intently at how little a prospective worker was prepared to work for, rather than at his or her ability to do the job.

Tom would have to start from scratch. Most of the production workers were not even aware of the existence of the useless sales staff. He had several abortive attempts before he succeeded in fostering a feeling of dislike amongst most of the production workers, but he finally hit upon a winning formula.

Taking the production workers collective passion for football as his starting point, he suggested that all the new sales staff were rugby supporters, who looked on football as a game for pansies. Football had a status well above religion within the polish production teams, and Dawes was sure that their obsession would be sufficient to establish ill-feelings. He further embellished the rumour later, by also suggesting that the sales team looked down their noses at overt displays of support for a team, as being intellectually unmanly. Dawes was proud of this latter supplement to the rumour, as it explained why such keen rugby supporters displayed no tokens of affiliation in their own office.

The rumour worked well, except in the Millwall supporting area.

This greatly surprised Tom Dawes, who thought their natural aggression would cause a rush to defend their chosen game. He had been concerned that his strategy might have invoked violence from this particularly difficult to manage team.

Dawes was not a student of Machiavelli, and his attempts at fostering change failed to take account of the natural behaviour of the crew. When the Millwall supporters heard the rumour, they took the view that whilst their own game was a wonderful excuse for violence on the terraces, rugby took the process a step further, and sanctified violence on the pitch as well. It encouraged bodily contact in a way that football did not, and by inference the inevitable results of such contact. Any game, played by heavily scarred, broken nosed, men, which permitted the shedding of blood, snot and teeth in the name of sport had to be admired.

It was an epiphany for some who realised that rugby could give them all the thrills of their beloved football, but without the danger of being cracked on the head by a brick, or flying beer bottle, whenever goals were scored in the Lion's Den. Most of them wore team caps as they stood on the terraces, carefully padded with old copies of the *Daily Mirror*.

In consequence, their workplace became a shrine to the red and black strip of Blackheath Rugby Club, as well as their traditional blue and white. Millwall production workers were to be seen in the canteen attempting to hold conversations with bewildered sales staff: who generally feared the blue and white clad workers, and usually contrived to keep a healthy distance from them.

Given that they were the most aggressive team, Tom was lost for a way to set them against the sales staff. Without the Millwall crew's support for the proposed change, it would have been a dangerous move to attempt to sack them. In addition, if the two groups spent much time together then the Millwall supporters would come to realise that the rumour was untrue. Things could go disastrously wrong.

But luck was on Tom's side.

A curly haired, stuttering, salesman named Oswald Winstanton, did what Dawes had failed to achieve. He confessed to a blue and white clad worker that he too was a football supporter, a fan of Accrington Stanley football club. This horrified the polish team. How could anyone support a team with such a chequered career: one that had recently closed its doors for two years, and finally re-emerged as a non-league side only a year ago. It showed a severe lack of judgement to support an obscure, distant, and decidedly down-market, club when there were such wonderful teams as Millwall on the doorstep. The revelation finally brought the blue and white's thinking in line with the other teams, and all further attempts at social contact were abandoned. All red and black paraphernalia was quietly removed, and the circumstances were right for the demise of excess sales staff.

Redundancy notices were issued to the six sales staff, given their relatively short service redundancy payments were a pittance, and the process less likely to be contested than sacking. Henry Fothergill organised this, and had a twinge of guilt about it. One of the six was a good worker, but to single him out would have been both contentious and risky.

Just as Tom and Tracey thought they had solved a problem, young Darren from dispatch upset their plans. Three of his loading bay staff had handed in their notice. They had formed a backing group for a friend, and were off in a beaten up old van, to play in pubs and clubs along the south coast.

Darren viewed their departure as no great loss. They had spent a lot of time singing badly, and using cardboard boxes as impromptu drum kits, to the detriment of the levels of wastage in the packaging area.

He had tried to recruit new staff, but without success. A few prospects had turned up, but for one reason or another he had not managed to secure the services of any of them. One had actually said that he would not work for somebody half his age, but most were either unsuitable, or not prepared to work for the wages offered.

In view of the impending departure of the six from sales, who were currently working out their notice, he asked if he could interview them as potential replacements. Henry and Tracey were reluctant to agree, but finally, after reviewing the excessive overtime that the remaining dispatch staff carried out to stay ahead of the orders placed, they gave in to the insistent Darren.

*****

Darren arranged his staff interviews for the Friday afternoon, once the afternoon delivery van was loaded, and the bay was quiet. His previous interviewer experiences were not happy ones, and as the day drew near he realised he had no real idea how to go about it. In panic he contacted his old boss, Gloria Ford, and asked for a few tips. She had been generous in her advice.

Today, armed with copious notes and a new tie, he sat in the empty room set aside for his task, and awaited the first candidate on his list.

"Come in!" he boomed confidently, in response to the timid knock on the door.

He looked up at the mousey haired girl who crept in, to stand in front of his desk. Then he looked down at his list, and shook his head.

"You're Richard Dickinson?" he asked incredulously.

"No, silly. Dickie is sleeping off lunch at his desk, so I thought I'd swap with him, and see you now instead of later. I'm Jenny Wellbeloved."

Darren looked at his list. There, third down: due at three-thirty. He put a little cross against the name at the top of the list and looked up with a smile.

"Sit down, Jenny. Now, there are two purposes for this interview. For me to see if you are capable of doing the job, and for you to understand what the work entails."

Darren smiled again. So far it was going okay. He studied the rather emaciated Jenny for a while. Jenny, meanwhile studied the room.

"The work involves making up orders from stores, and deciding which method of dispatch the order will require. Some of the orders are quite heavy. How do you feel about lugging big boxes about all day?"

While Darren was speaking, Jenny had been gazing around the room rather vacantly.

"You could do with some new curtains on that window, or perhaps one of those roller blind thingies. Sorry, what were you saying?"

"I was asking how you felt about lifting heavy boxes."

"And a nice blue carpet would make the room look bigger. Sorry, did you say something?"

Darren breathed in, and counted to ten.

"Can you stop studying the room for a minute. Just long enough for me to establish if you are suitable for a job on the loading bay."

"Sorry, I was thinking one of those wood and glass Swedish light fittings would go nicely with the blue carpet. Did you say that you thought I was suitable for the job? Oh, thank you. Will this be my office?"

Darren decided that counting to ten again would not be adequate to control his feelings. He would go down to the canteen, and come back later for his next interview. He would ask Personnel to write to Jenny telling her she had not got the job. Perhaps she concentrated better on written communications.

As he opened the door, Jenny turned and smiled at him. It was the sort of smile that the runt of the litter in the pet shop window uses, when trying to get picked for a new home.

"Start on Monday, at eight o'clock," he said weakly.

"Oh, thank you. Granny will be pleased."

As Darren left Jenny, who returned to gazing at the walls and muttering about Regency Stripes, her last remark triggered something in his mind. It was only a small trigger, but it had something to do with a discussion that he once overheard in the queue in the canteen: a discussion about the over-generous distribution of grandmothers to some families.

Sitting in the canteen afterwards, with a mug of Edith's foul tea, did nothing to ease Darren's mind. He had conducted his first staff interview of the day, and failed miserably. He was determined to do better with the second candidate. He glanced at his watch, sighed, and stood up to return to the interview room. As he walked towards the stairs, the stomach rumble, familiar to all consumers of Edith's brew, made him change direction for the door marked 'Gents' at the far end of the room.

When Darren eventually arrived back at the interview room, some five minutes late for his next appointment, he found a short, chubby man of about thirty sitting in his chair behind the desk. He was reading Darren's interview preparation notes. As Darren entered the room the man ignored him, so he coughed. The man looked up.

"Hepworth's the name," said the man, pointing at the second line on Darren's list. "So you're employing us as dispatch clerks. Bit of a let-down after being a sales executive, but I suppose I could stay on if the money was right."

Darren, whose confidence had grown as the memory of his first interview faded, glared at the man.

"That's my chair, and I'm interviewing you as a candidate for a position. I will decide if you are suitable for the job or not."

Hepworth looked up, obviously puzzled by Darren's opening statement, and then back at the notes spread out on the desk. He remained in possession of the chair.

"It says here 'set the candidate at ease'; I don't think you handled that very well. Do you? And turning up late don't exactly give a good impression either."

Darren began to realise why Tracey had been so keen to get rid of the sales staff. The thought struck him that he had another four to go. His mind went blank, and he desperately wanted to consult the notes that he had left on the desk. He reached forward, snatched them up, and stood in front of his sitting interviewee.

"The job," he said falteringly, "the job involves packing and lifting heavy boxes. All day long!"

He wanted to add, '*standing on your feet, not sitting in my chair*', but Darren was a well brought up young man, and considered such words too impolite.

Hepworth blinked.

"I'll take the job. I can start on Tuesday. Monday is my day to go fishing. I always take Monday off. It helps to relieve the stresses of work."

Darren glanced at his notes. Right at the top of the page Gloria had reminded him that he was in charge, and that he should be firm. As his rage rose quickly from a gentle simmer to a rapid boil Darren exploded.

"I don't think you are suitable for this position, Mr Hepworth. In fact, I'm not sure that you are suitable for any position that involves doing what you are told to do. Good day!"

He opened the door to signify that the interview was at an end. But Hepworth stayed seated.

"Goodbye!" hinted Darren as he held the door wide open.

"No need to be like that. Out of the goodness of my heart I was prepared to take your miserable job. I even thought I could make some improvements to the place. But if you don't recognise talent then I'll take myself elsewhere."

"Please do!"

Hepworth ambled out, and Darren took possession of his warm chair. He was determined not to vacate it again until the last candidate left the building. On his list he saw Jenny Wellbeloved scheduled next. Having already hired her, he had a gap in his schedule: time he could use to think happy thoughts and compose himself.

But Darren was not fated to enjoy the comfort of his chair for long. Edith's brew took one last grip at his internals, and he had to dash along the corridor. Eventually he felt sufficiently physically and mentally composed, and returned to the room, with an ominous feeling in the pit of his stomach that could have been either fear of what was to come, or a last goodbye from Edith's tea.

He entered the room, and left the door open. More welcoming, to set the candidate at ease, he thought.

"Good day to you, Mr Darren, Sir."

The voice caught Darren off guard. As he had opened the door it had swung back and masked the man standing against the wall. He spun round to face whatever ordeal he was about to endure. To his relief he saw a broad grinning pink face: generously freckled and topped with a shock of red hair. The man stood slightly stooped forward in a servile manner.

Darren recognised him, or rather knew him to be one of two men he had seen in the canteen. Obviously twins, and always seen together. He sat, and motioned for the man to occupy a chair in front of the desk.

"Tank you, Mr Darren, Sir. I'm a bit early, sir. I saw dat Hepworth fellow come back, and so I knew dat you were free, so I just slipped along. I tink it's better to be early than late. So it is, to be sure, Sir."

Darren consulted his list. There were two entries with the same surname: William and Patrick O'Keefe.

"And you are?"

"William O'Keefe is my God given name, if it pleases you, Mr Darren, Sir. But I'm called Billy by my friends."

"Well, Billy!" said Darren, remembering his note to set the candidate at ease. "And what makes you think that you are suitable for a job in dispatch?"

"I like working with people, Sir. My brother, now he's good with the paperwork, but I prefer to do tings with me hands, Sir. I don't mind heavy work, Sir. I was brought up on my Grandpa's farm. Heaving the potatoes about all day, so I was, to be sure."

Darren paused, waiting for the inevitable 'sir' that Billy used to terminate most sentences. But it never came.

"Well, Billy. You clearly can do the physical work. You say that your brother's good with paperwork, but what about you? There's quite a bit of paperwork in filling orders, and creating dispatch labels."

"Ah, well, there you have me, Sir. The ting is, if I work with Pat then we get along just fine, Sir. He makes sure of dat. But on me own, like, I struggle a bit with the letters. On the farm, if Grandpa needed help he kept me home, 'cause Pat's the clever one, sir. He suited the schooling."

"But you've been working in sales. Surely that involved a lot of paperwork?"

"Ah, sure it did, it did indeed, Mr Darren, Sir. But I'm all right with the numbers, and Pat would make me a list for the telephone. And as I said, Sir, I like working with people. The talking to them was no bother at all, at all."

Darren felt he needed Solomon's judgement skills. He liked Billy. He was honest to a fault, and clearly more than capable of heaving boxes around all day. If only he could be sure that they would end up with the right customers. He decided to take a chance.

"Can you start on Monday, Billy?"

"Dat I can gladly, Mr Darren, Sir."

"We begin at eight o'clock in dispatch, and finish at four."

Billy broke into a broad grin.

"Dat's just grand, Mr Darren, Sir."

"I'll see you on Monday then, Billy. Goodbye."

Darren stood up, and held his hand out, to find it gripped eagerly in a ham-like fist. His newest worker turned to leave, but paused at the door, with a worried expression on his face. Darren guessed the reason why.

"Tell Pat that he's got a job too, if he wants it. And Billy, if Pat does want the job, then see Oswald Winstanton and tell him that all the positions have been filled."

"Dat I will, Mr Darren, Sir. With pleasure, Sir. Tank you."

Darren sighed as he watched Billy leave. He had taken his first real step into management, and felt that on balance he had handled it well. He was particularly pleased with how he had delegated the task of telling Winstanton the bad news to Billy. The man was clearly capable of handling the consequences of how Winstanton took his message, and no doubt his brother would be there to support him. Darren walked back to the loading bay, confident that he had made the right decisions.

A swaying Dickinson arrived at the loading bay as Darren was tidying up before going home.

"I'm sorry I missed my appointment," he said as he stood, one hand on a stack of parcels for support. "I got involved in something, and forgot the time. But I'm here now!"

Darren looked at him, and sniffed the distillery fumes that he expelled with each breath. He winced as the man swayed closer and exhaled directly at him.

"The jobs have all been taken, and I understand that you were asleep at your desk when you should have been seeing me. I need reliable staff working for me, and if you can't stay sober on a day that you have a job interview then clearly you do not fit that description."

Darren stared at the man, and waited for his words to sink in. Dickinson opened his mouth to reply, but either thought better of it or else his befuddled brain failed to find suitable words. He stood there imitating a hungry goldfish, before turning and shambling off, leaving Darren in charge of his domain, and feeling that he had done a good day's work. Darren gathered up his interview notes and headed towards the Personnel Office to tell them of his decisions, confident that he had solved his staffing shortage and chosen the best of the bunch to join his team.

In the office Betty greeted him with the sort of smile one gives to soldiers returning battered and bruised from a dangerous mission.

"How did you get on?"

"Okay, I've selected these three," said Darren proudly.

Betty looked at Darren's list, with three names heavily crossed out, and neat little ticks against the others.

"Really?" queried Betty. "Including her?"

Darren nodded and left. As he walked back downstairs he had the distinct feeling that there was something that someone was not telling him.

3. THE BEST LAID PLANS OF WOMEN

Asking around amongst her wide circle of men-friends, Tracey Mulligan soon found a contact who could recommend an industrial chemist. The man in question owned a chemist's shop. He once also had a very profitable sideline, manufacturing condoms for local barbers to sell, but relaxing public attitudes to sex resulted in a high street chain of chemists openly selling cheaper products from a national rubber company.

Gone were the days when population control relied on the barber prompting his customers with a discrete 'Anything for the weekend, sir?' as he brushed the loose hairs from their shoulders and collar. Reliance on this time honoured discrete custom would, in any case, be less effective in an age of long-haired hippies for whom the barber was an alien concept.

Potter still had a small dedicated group of customers who preferred a quality, locally made, product, but the mass market that he once filled had either opted for cheaper supplies from sources on the high street, or taken to newer forms of contraceptive.

Potter ran a one-man chemist shop during the day, so Tracey arranged to meet him in *The Squinting Badger* one evening. After buying him a drink, and a few minutes general chat about her problem of falling demand, Tracey broached the main purpose of the meeting. Alfred Potter, who had good cause to be very familiar with the problem of falling demand, nodded sagely as she spoke.

"Well, Mr Potter, I understand that you know all there is to know about making paint. I need to come up with a new line. One that trades on our reputation for quality, but is aimed at a new market."

Tracey smiled at the stocky little man with a Kaiser moustache sitting opposite her. He looked every bit the corner shop chemist.

"I don't know everything, Miss Mulligan, but certainly enough to develop a line of basic paint for domestic use. It only really needs a pigment, an adhesive and a bulking agent. My real expertise is in the area of pigments and chemical reactions."

"I need something a bit different; something not currently available that we can develop a market for."

"A specialist paint then," mused Potter. "Something that does a job not well covered at the moment. That's a bit of a challenge, Miss Mulligan. First we need to create the product, and then we must generate a market for it. But I do have a few ideas."

Tracey was about to reply when, to her surprise, she saw a rather ashen faced Henry Fothergill put his head round the door, and scan the customers. When he spotted her, his face relaxed a little, and he marched towards them at an unusually fast pace.

"Herbert Strudwick has woken up!"

"What?"

"Herbert Strudwick has woken up. Lionel Dee phoned me at home, and I've been looking for you all over Peckham."

"But the man's been in a coma for almost two years. The last time anyone spoke of him, they said he was getting weaker. They hinted that he was slowly slipping away."

"Well, he's not slipping away now. The only slipping he's doing is his hand round the waists of the nurses who tend him. He's awake, and demanding to know what's happened to his company."

She turned back to face Potter.

"I'm sorry Mr Potter, but something urgent has cropped up. I'll contact you in a day or so, but you know the broad outline of what I want to do: an innovative product that fits with our existing range. Perhaps you could do a few cost calculations and a short feasibility report for me. I'll make it worth your while."

She smiled as she spoke.

Potter nodded avidly. Tracey had in mind a consultancy fee, but her words, and that smile, caused Potter to interpret her remark differently. Whenever the opportunity arose, he had always been an enthusiastic user of his own product range.

"Now Henry, how does this affect us? Surely the sale of the factory to Hardcastle severed any connection that the factory might have had with the Strudwick family."

"I wish that were true. The sale was partly funded by converting Strudwick shares into Hardcastle stock. Most of the Strudwick family then sold their holdings, before Hardcastle worked out the true state of affairs, but..."

Henry hesitated.

"Well, what is it?"

"Because he was in a coma, Herbert Strudwick's shares were held in trust, and got overlooked. He is still a shareholder in Hardcastles."

"But surely his shares were set aside to pay for his care?"

"No. Since he was in the factory, and in the company of an employee, his fall was classed as an industrial accident. The company has been paying his hospice fees, out of pre-tax profits. Apparently they paid them three months in advance. I only found out myself some months after Hardcastle took over, when we got a final demand for non-payment, threatening to switch off his life support systems. Our continued payments to the hospice imply accepting responsibility for the man, and an ongoing financial relationship."

There was no need for Henry to explain further. Herbert Strudwick's loss of balance, whilst at the height of servicing his attractive assistant on his flimsy office desk, was a legend in Peckham, one that grew with every retelling.

"Well! In one sense, he was certainly on the job, but I would not have thought that it could have been interpreted as such in the commercial sense."

She grinned as she pictured the incident. "How does it affect us?"

"He wants to come back to work when he is fit enough."

"But that must be to the Strudwick Sausage Company at Goose Green, surely?"

"He seems anxious to return to Gordon Road. Lionel Dee went to see him, and he kept asking if there had been any structural changes to the building. Lionel told me that he had grown up in one of the houses."

"Perhaps I should go and visit him. What do you think?"

For the first time that she could remember Henry chuckled, and a smile spread across his handsome face. He was imagining the effect she would have on the randy old man.

"From what I hear about him, he would enjoy that. But wear plimsolls, and be prepared to run. I hear he used to be rather lively on his feet as far as young ladies were concerned."

"I'm not so very young, Henry."

"In Herbert's case, *young* was a relative term. And, if you do not mind me saying so, you are an extremely attractive woman."

He laughed nervously. She had never heard him laugh before. Suddenly she saw what his wife Jane could see in him: a totally dependable, but rather private, man who reserved his sense of humour to share with those he felt most comfortable with.

Tracey had made it a policy to never interpose in a truly happy marriage, but in Henry's case she would be prepared to make an exception. However, she doubted that he would.

"I'll phone Lionel, and arrange for you to visit Herbert with him. Meanwhile I think I need to take another look at the sales agreement from Strudwick to Hardcastle."

Henry sat back glumly, and carefully rested his hands on a dry patch of the sticky table between them. He stayed silently thinking for a few minutes as Tracey finished her Campari and Soda. She drained the last dregs, and put down her glass.

"Have a drink, Henry. What will it be?"

Henry looked at his watch. He was too late to see his children before bedtime, and perhaps Jane would have cooled down if he left it a while. She had not been pleased when, after the phone call from Lionel Dee, he had dashed out to find Tracey.

"A large brandy, please!"

Tracey made her way to the crowded bar, where she quickly caught the attention of the barman, despite the queue of other customers already waiting to be served. She returned shortly after with his drink, and another Campari and soda for herself.

"Nobody ever expected old Herbert to recover," said Henry after taking a slow thoughtful sip at his drink.

"Lionel told me that a new student nurse had been assigned to look after him, and she would sit and read to her patient. Others had done that before, but this girl had got hold of a copy of *Lady Chatterley's Lover* and, assuming the comatose patient was beyond hearing, had read selected passages out loud, imagining the scenes with him and her as the two main characters. She was also not above whispering rude suggestions to him, as she took his pulse and washed him.

It seems that the old rascal responded to her, and she began to notice small movements of his fingers when she spoke. This encouraged her to be more graphic in her conversations, and to make extended physical contact when tending to his needs. Suddenly one day he opened his eyes, and made a feeble grab for her as she bent to straighten his sheets.

After that he has rapidly made progress in muscle strength and movement. So much so that when Lionel phoned me they had assigned his personal care to male nurses only. "

Tracey watched Henry's face as he spoke. There was not a hint of emotion as he recounted the more colourful aspects of the story. He simply told the facts as if in a witness box.

Eventually the implication of him spending the evening drinking with Tracey, or at least Jane's interpretation of the implication, got the better of him.

"Time I was off. Jane will be wondering where I've got to."

"Give her my regards," said Tracey.

Henry nodded, but decided that the less he mentioned her name at home the better. As he stepped out onto the pavement he saw the junior storeman, Swinton, enter the Indian restaurant across the road with a slim blonde girl and a man he recognised, but could not place.

As he got into his car the man's name came to him. Detective Constable Holmes! No, not Detective Constable, he had heard that Holmes had been promoted since he last saw him.

★ The Star in the East ★ Top Hole Indian Cuisine ★

4. A NEW LEASE OF LIFE

Tracey Mulligan wore her least flattering business suit for her visit to Herbert Strudwick, but there was no hiding her hourglass figure and stunningly beautiful face. Lionel Dee, the Strudwicks accountant, picked her up from the factory. Stanley Capes was with him, and the three of them chatted about their respective businesses on the way to St Borgia's. Tracey got the impression that Lionel and Stanley had a much better idea of the true financial state of the factory than the current owner, Sebastian Hardcastle.

At St Borgia's they found a stout matronly figure already at the man's bedside. Herbert was arguing with her when they arrived. She was clearly pleased to have an excuse to turn away from him, and greet his visitors.

"Hello Lionel, Stanley, and you must be Tracey Mulligan. I've heard a lot about you," said the woman warmly. "I'm Catherine, Herbert's sister."

The emaciated patient was propped up on a pile of pillows. His dull eyes lit up as Tracey approached, and he suspended his argument with his sister to watch her. He stared for some time, taking in every detail from her long blonde hair down to her shapely calves and trim ankles, but mainly concentrating in the upper regions. His nose twitched as *Evening in Paris* took over from bleach and floor polish as the dominant aroma.

"You've stolen my factory! But I'm still in charge," he whispered in a voice that had not, until recently, been used for two years.

"Hello, Mr Strudwick. I'm so pleased to see you on the mend. It must be strange to have two years removed from your life like that."

Lionel noticed that Tracey deliberately ignored the remark about the factory. He watched the old man strain to look down her blouse, as she leant forward to place a bunch of flowers, and a bottle of Lucozade, on his locker. Clearly two years in a coma had not had much of an impact upon his character: perhaps he thought he had a lot of catching up to do.

Tracey smiled at the patient, and stood back upright, much to his obvious disappointment.

"Didn't you hear what I said? You've stolen my factory."

"Yes I did hear, and I chose to ignore it, as it is far from the truth of what has happened in your absence. Your family very wisely chose to sell out to Sebastian Hardcastle when they found that certain economic changes were adversely affecting them. Since then I have taken a half share in the Gordon Road business. I believe that you now have a five percent interest in the 'Hardcastle Cattle, Cake and Pie Co-op', which gives you a one percent share in the Gordon Road factory.

As a shareholder I would welcome your input, although as a previous owner I must point out that you were heading for bankruptcy, and that would throw a question mark over the value of any advice you care to offer."

Out of the corner of her eye she saw Catherine turn towards the window to hide a smirk. She doubted that any woman had ever spoken to Herbert that way before.

"Miss Strudwick. I believe you are an accountant. Can you explain to your brother the implication of what has happened while he has lain unconscious?"

"It's Mrs Humber, Mrs Samuel Humber, actually. But yes, I've already tried to explain to him. Perhaps in time he will come to understand."

"Thank you, Catherine, and I'm sorry. I was not aware you were married."

"Last Saturday. I should be on my honeymoon in Bruges, but for a telegram about Herbert."

Catherine blushed as she spoke, and held out a hand with a shiny gold band and a little diamond ring as evidence to support her statement.

"I am still the owner." interrupted Herbert, clearly annoyed that his sister had distracted his shapely visitor's attention from himself. "The factory has a ninety nine year lease, and I own the freehold! You can't make any alterations without my say so. Do you hear me?"

All four turned to look at the frail old man in the bed. Then Tracey moved her head towards Catherine, and raised her eyebrows.

"It's news to me."

Herbert cackled.

"I'll be round to inspect my property, just as soon as I'm up and about."

As the old man continued to feast his eyes on his delightful visitor, it was apparent to all that the factory premises were not the only thing he would like to inspect. Tracey could see no reason to stay any longer.

"It was nice to meet you, Mrs Humber. My hearty congratulations on your marriage. Perhaps, once your brother has adjusted himself to the facts, we might meet socially, in more convivial circumstances."

Catherine shook the offered hand, and then stepped closer to kiss Tracey on both cheeks. More than a quarter of a century later, and with a new man in her life, yet she still held on to a continental habit learnt during those mad few months of summer and autumn 1940.

Tracey made her way back to the factory, and looked in on Henry Fothergill.

"How did it go?"

"Not sure. I think he may come to terms with not being a part of the company, but he claims that he owns the freehold of the place, and we need his say so to make any changes."

"Are you sure? I thought the factory was freehold. I remember Hardcastle gloating about the property being a valuable asset."

"I've only got his word for it. Can you look into it for me?"

"Okay boss."

He grinned.

'That's the second time this week,' thought Tracey, as she returned his grin with a smile.

5. A FLEXIBLE NEW APPROACH

"There's a Mr Potter to see you."

"Thank you, Susan. Could you call Mr Derry and Mr Dawes and ask them to join us, then could you arrange some tea...? On second thoughts forget the tea. Get a pot of coffee sent up."

'I really must do something about Edith's tea,' thought Tracey, as she tidied her desk, and turned to face the opening door.

"Welcome, Mr Potter... Alfred. May I ask you to make yourself comfortable while we wait for two of my staff to join us?"

Potter came into the room, shed his raincoat and sought the chair beside her desk. He had barely settled when Tom Dawes arrived, closely followed by Reg Swinton. Tracey raised an eyebrow at the junior storeman.

"Harry's been off with lumbago all week Miss. But he's told me what you are planning, and I'm to take notes and report back."

She nodded. It was a nuisance, but she doubted that his absence at this stage was critical. Once both men were ready, she outlined her plan and asked Potter to tell her what he had come up with so far.

"As I see it, you need a paint that is in demand, but not currently available. My main expertise has been with rubber goods, so I wondered about a rubber-based paint. I think as a specialist product it would sit better with your existing range than a mass-volume, low profit margin paint. I doubt that you could compete with Woolworth in the short term."

Tracey frowned.

"There are a number of applications for rubber based paints, including washable bathroom walls and floors, felt roof resealing, damp-proofing, outside walls, marine equipment and electrics, and many others."

"But you can already buy rubberised paint. I use it on the whitewall tyres on my Consul," said Tom Dawes.

"Yes! But only in a few basic colours, and using a chlorinated base: not something you would want to use in any quantity indoors. I propose a latex water based solution, much safer in a confined space. Besides, because of the pigments I've experimented with on my other products, I can make a much wider range, and cheaply at that. I have a few samples in my briefcase. With all these hippies about, you could even sell pre-painted flower power tents, or stencil kits for the more creative bearded weirdy."

Potter clicked open the case. Inside were half a dozen hardboard panels each painted with little squares in a multitude of shades of colour. Every square of paint was neatly labelled with a name of Potter's choosing.

"*Passionate Pink*," he said, proudly pointing to a particularly bright shade, "and there is *Bordello Brown, Marital Maroon, Frigid Blue, Valentine Yellow, Pleasure-me Purple*."

He reeled off the names of more than a dozen colours, all names clearly invented to encourage sales of his barbers' supplies.

"*Baby-Doll Red*," murmured Reg with a shudder, as he spotted a lurid shade that reminded him of a hulk of an ex-girlfriend called Mabel.

Tom looked at the square marked *Reeperbahn Red,* and then at Reg with a quizzical expression.

"You had to be there," said Reg by way of explanation, and winced at the memory of Mabel skimpily clad in red nylon baby-doll pyjamas.

Tom nodded, and read across the square of blues and purples.

"*Easy Violet?*"

"It's a long story," said Potter dreamily.

"Sounds more like a short story, if she was that easy," said Tom with a smirk.

Tracey put down the square of green shades, and looked at Potter. Despite the ribald naming of the colours the man was stern faced: clearly a man who was serious about business, and knew the value of appropriate advertising.

"Have you done much testing of the actual paints, Alfred?"

"Certainly. I've painted a number of surfaces, and would be happy to show you them back at my workshop."

Potter smiled at Tracey. He was particularly thinking of his bedroom windowsill and bed headboard as he spoke.

"How durable is it? Can it be scrubbed? I'm thinking of an alternative to tiles in a bathroom or kitchen."

"No need! A gentle wipe is all that is necessary. But there is another aspect to it. You can make a simple frame, cover it in cardboard and then apply three coats to make a durable rubber wall. A complete shed for little more than the cost of the paint, and a few sheets of cardboard. For a more solid structure use hardboard. The paint is totally waterproof once dry. You could even build out of Weetabix. I have a young niece who has an outdoor rabbit hutch roofed with cornflake packets."

Tom and Reg exchanged glances, but neither dared ask Potter which particular suggestively named colour would be suitable for the home of a little girl's pet.

Building materials had been in short supply with so much post-war reconstruction going on, and that had put up the price of good timber. But the factory was awash with cardboard packaging. Tom Dawes smiled as he thought of a little shed for his back yard. Something in *Seductive Green*, with a *Frigid Blue* roof, and *Nympho Grey* detailing.

"There's just one problem," said Potter. "At the moment I can only make small batches, say four gallons at a time. Anything larger and the mix starts to get lumpy. I think I can solve that with accurate temperature control, but it's not something I've had to worry about with my existing products."

Tracey looked at Dawes.

"I don't see that as a problem at this stage. The French polish production runs are only five gallons a batch, and it means we could use existing equipment for trial batches."

She smiled.

"Tom, why don't you take Alfred along, and show him the production areas? Then perhaps the pair of you could join me for lunch downstairs in an hour or so. You can leave your case here Alfred, it will be quite safe."

The two men got up to leave, and Reg rose also.

"Would you wait a minute, Reg. I might have need of your special skills."

He sat down again, and watched Tracey as she shuffled papers on her desk. The only 'special skills' he had related to his criminal past, and he was hoping that he had put those behind him. As soon as the door closed she looked up, and smiled. He recognised that smile. It was delightfully seductive, but he normally saw it just before she gave him an instruction that put his freedom at risk.

"It's been a while since we had a chat, Piggy," she said, reverting to the nickname that the uniformed officers at Peckham Police Station had given him.

"How are you enjoying honest work? It must be hard running that flat all on your own. By the way, I see from our Personnel records that you are classed as a junior trainee. That was a mean trick by Ponsonby, so you'll find on Friday that your wages have gone up a bit and you are now graded as a storeman."

Reg gazed at her. In the past, just looking at her made his knees go weak, and other bodily parts stiffen, but now, as a result of frequent exposure, the effect was less pronounced. He returned the smile, and sat more upright.

"Thank you. The job's okay. I like working with Harry, and I'm not on my own. Maria, I mean Mary, has come back from Devon now the Ernshaw gang are mostly locked up. She's been staying with me."

Tracey studied Piggy for a few moments before speaking. The permissive society had made much progress in the past decade, but not within the probation service where co-habiting was still looked on as something to be severely discouraged. Especially between parolees and known criminals.

"Really, Piggy? And what does John Dillon say about that?"

"It's not like that. We're just friends, and in any case there was never anything proved against her."

Tracey listened to what he said, and continued to watch him intently. Despite his growing resistance to her charms, as her perfume crept into his nostrils her presence was beginning to affect him. He squirmed in his chair, to make himself more comfortable.

"Have you heard that Herbert Strudwick has regained consciousness?"

He nodded.

"Well, he claims he owns the freehold of the factory. I've got Henry Fothergill looking into it, but it might be easier if you take a peek for me."

Deja vu hit Piggy, and whilst he stiffened his resolve not to commit any more burglaries for her, that smile and perfume took full effect and stiffened more physical body parts. He knew he was powerless to resist.

"I'll need to find out where he's likely to keep the documents, and speak to you in a few days' time. Oh, and by the way, is Mary working? I've heard she's an excellent cook, and the canteen could do with a bit of a shake up."

Piggy thought for a moment. Currently Mary was helping out on a market fruit stall for a neighbour who had suffered serious chest injuries, but that was likely to come to an end soon. Especially if it ever became known that he sustained his injuries from another acquaintance of Reg. His previous girlfriend, Mabel, was currently serving time in Holloway for battering the man in a drunken rage, but somehow his friendly local police station had managed to keep her relationship to Reg secret.

"I'll ask her if she is interested."

"When does Mabel get out?"

Piggy grinned.

"Not a problem. I got a letter from her saying she was sorry to break our engagement, and my heart, but she had found someone else."

"In Holloway?"

"Her cousin Keith thinks it might be a prison visitor. She wrote to her parents saying she was moving to Watford when she was released. According to her family it's a great relief to them all. They prefer their violence to be coldly calculated in the ring, not drink inspired."

"I'm sure John Dillon will be very relieved to hear it. I understand that you are being quoted down at the Probation Service Office as the success story of the year. I don't think he was looking forward to supervising Mabel upon her release."

Piggy smiled as he remembered his probation officer, Dillon, witnessing Piggy's attempt at evicting Mabel from his home: an attempt that she interpreted as a proposal of marriage. Piggy still had occasional nightmares about Mabel. He glanced at his watch.

"I must be off. I've got the bottling run to batch up, and the Millwall team are hell to work with after a home defeat."

Each of the polish production groups supported a different football team. Their work-places were decorated with posters and photographs of the teams, and they wore clothing in their team colours. They also adopted the crowd behaviour of their team's supporters. The cleaners and porters had once asked if they could be issued with spray cans of tear gas when visiting some particularly notorious workshops.

"You take care now, Piggy. Any news of when Mr Derry will be back?"

"He sent in a sick note for a fortnight, but I went to see him last night. He hopes to come back before then."

"Do you need any help in the stores? I could ask Darren to lend you a dispatcher."

Piggy shook his head. Recently a number of dispatch staff had been replaced, and there were now some very odd characters on the loading bay. This week it had sprouted window boxes, and hanging baskets. A few days ago, when he had cause to visit the bay, he had interrupted an argument between the dispatch supervisor and one of his new staff. Darren was trying to explain why he did not think that blue carpet on the concrete floor of the loading bay would be a good idea, and did not appear to be convincing the mousey-haired girl he was talking to. Darren might have had more success if he could have kept her attention on the conversation. At the time she was watering a hanging basket of spiky grass-like plants that dripped on a stack of packing cases.

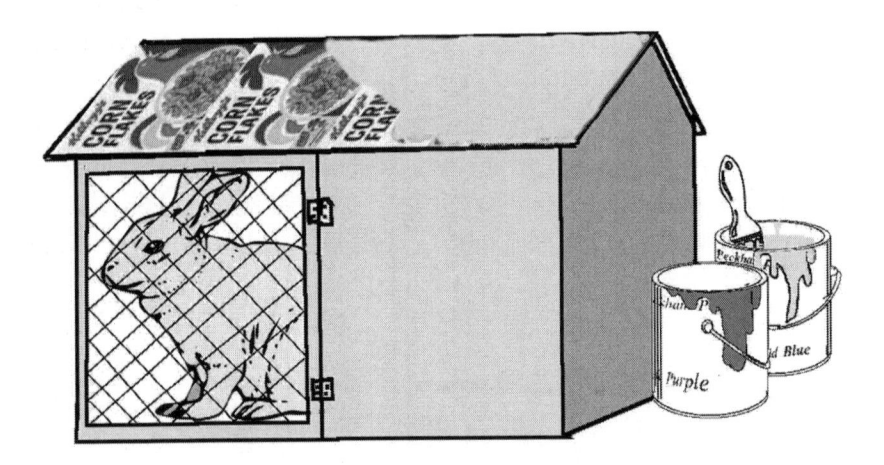

6. INDUSTRIAL COHESION

Alfred Potter applied himself to the task of planning a large-scale production process for latex rubber paint with great energy. Almost as much energy as he put into pursuing anything in a skirt that crossed his path on his visits to the factory. Paradoxically, once terms of employment had been agreed, only the lovely Tracey was immune to his attentions, presumably on the grounds of him not wishing to jeopardise himself financially.

The existing production area was made up of eight independent teams in eight separate areas, each making a slightly different shade of French Polish, and supporting a different football team.

In consultation with Tom Dawes, Tracey chose the Wolverhampton Wanderers supporting team to convert to rubber paint production. They made a rather reddish shade of polish, in marked contrast to the gold and black clothing they all wore, which Tom said could be imitated by mixing two shades from the other teams. They were also some of the youngest workers, which Tom hoped would make them the most adaptable to new processes. He should have realised their adherence to a team which had a glorious past, and a doubtful future, did not suggest minds open to change.

The team ceased polish production, and began to set up for pilot production of the new product. Alfred Potter joined the staff to supervise the work, and produced a little training booklet for the team to read before they started working with the materials involved.

All went well until he brought in the materials and recipes, to make the first trial batches. On the first day of mixing, one of the young polish stirrers arrived with a note from his mother forbidding him from working on four of the most graphically named colours. The other stirrer refused to wear the facemask that Alfred provided to use when mixing the liquid chemicals that reacted to make the rubber solution. He claimed that it made him look foolish. Potter argued in vain that the masks made them look like the handsome lead in the television series Doctor Kildare, but the pair were adamant that looked more like Kenneth Williams and Frankie Howerd in the film Carry on Doctor.

Fred Parkinson, the room charge-hand, broke the habit of a lifetime, and had an inspirational thought.

"Could we make the masks gold and black?" he asked.

Both stirrers nodded eagerly. The younger one was prepared to ignore his mother's concern for his moral welfare, if he could work in his team's colours.

Potter made a note to make up some masks in the appropriate colours, and suggested that they also add the team motif to their overalls. If he could borrow one of the football posters he would make a wolf's head stencil, and apply the motif as soon as they made a batch of haystack gold. This trivial gesture immediately won Potter two highly enthusiastic, if incompetent, assistants. Fred was puzzled by 'Haystack Gold', given the more suggestive names of the others.

"T'was a September afternoon, and she was a farmer's daughter. I forget her name, but her hair exactly matched the colour of the stack we were in," said Potter by way of explanation.

With his two eager assistants looking on, Alfred Potter set to work and produced the very first batch on his own: four gallons of negligee black.

"It's the simplest to make," Potter said when asked why he did not start with one of the shades not available elsewhere. It also happened to be inspired by the night attire of his latest paramour.

Tom Dawes had ordered a crate of wide mouthed tins to store the paint, and Potter ladled the product carefully in. By lunchtime, a neat stack of anonymous shiny tins were ready to move to the stores.

In the past, Reg and Harry had collected each room's output separately, and placed it on dedicated shelving for labelling. But now one room would be creating various colours, and, at the outset, without any external indication of the contents.

This problem became apparent on the first batch. Reg went up to receive the tins. In the room a transistor radio competed with the noise of machinery in its assault on the ears. He spotted the youngest stirrer, who was in the process of filling his mouth with spam and piccalilli sandwich, and enquired as to what colour the tins contained.

The answer, conditioned by generations of job demarcation and restrictive practice, was a barely distinct mumble, "Ask Fred."

Reg, familiar with the bawdy naming convention of Potter's samples, duly took the tins back to stores and carefully labelled them with a coloured china-graph pencil, *Arse Red*.

At this point the company had not yet got paper labels for the product. They used a local printer to make the polish labels, and the design had not changed for several years. When Strudwick ran the company, they had a graphic designer in their marketing department, to design packaging for their sausages, but he had left with most of the other useful members of the workforce.

Henry Fothergill, not having been party to the discussions with Potter, said that his oldest child showed great promise as an artist. However, when he saw the colour names offered by Potter he withdrew his suggestion that the girl could be of help to them. He had to consult his wife, Jane, about the meaning of one name, to which she suggested that a demonstration would be more enlightening than a verbal description. It was a lengthy demonstration, repeated nightly for a week. Henry was late arriving at work each day of that week, and broke the habit of a lifetime of working late, to scurry home as early as possible every night.

Each day, Potter supervised making a batch of a different colour. Reg collected, and labelled, them without further mishap. On the Friday morning, Harry came in for a while to catch up on what was happening. He took one look at the labels Reg had taped to the shelves of rubber paint, and shook his head.

"We can't use names like that. We'd be a laughing stock."

Reg agreed.

"Has anyone ordered any labels yet?"

"No! Who would normally do that?"

"Me!" said Harry.

"I know Fothergill was hoping to get his daughter to design something," said Reg, "until he saw the colour names."

Harry laughed.

"I think I'd better go and have a word with the boss," he said, as he pulled out a handkerchief to clear his nose, and maximise his anticipated enjoyment of her perfume.

Harry found Tracey in the outer management office, with two newish clerical assistants. The dim, but physically attractive, help from Ponsonby's era had been replaced by women with excellent shorthand speed, good telephone manners and much inherent common sense.

One was cutting out a Butterick jacket pattern in what looked like old flannel sheeting, whilst Tracey and the other assistant were carefully painting the cut panels in Marital Maroon and Passionate Pink. She looked up and smiled as he entered. Harry felt the immediately. It was a feeling he thought he had abandoned years ago.

"Having fun?"

"Certainly not," giggled Tracey. "We're experimenting with new products. Waterproof fashionable clothes. Mary Quant's not the only one with new ideas."

"If you're busy I'll come back on Monday," said Harry, although he was reluctant to leave. He enjoyed watching the three of them as they cut and splashed paint about. He wondered if his pleasure at watching them work was what he and his wife would have felt, had they borne children to watch over as they grew into adulthood.

"No, Susan and Polly can finish this. Come into the office, Harry."

Harry warmed as he heard his name. It was only a foolish old man's whim, for Tracey had not singled him out for this familiar form of address. She had found that men responded to her better if she used first names, or better still nicknames. And she liked men to respond to her.

Here in the factory, the change in the atmosphere since her arrival had been quite dramatic. The familiarity had spread throughout a generation of normally repressed individuals. She often stood at her office window when the evening whistle blew, and counted the couples leaving hand in hand. The count increased weekly.

"Now, what can I do for you?"

Harry wondered if he really was too old to take a chance, but remembered his bad back just in time to stop from making a fool of himself.

"I think we have a problem with the names of the new paint colours, Miss."

"Please, call me Tracey. And don't worry. I'm just indulging Potter while we put together a full range. Once we agree on the product formulae I'm sure Potter will see reason and succumb to the lure of money. I was hoping to see you Harry. I understand that you manage the labelling."

"Yes," he replied cautiously.

"Can you speak to our printers, and see what they can do for us. I was thinking about a basic label with a separate sticky insert to name each colour. And we will need to have colour charts printed as well."

Harry thought for a while. He used a small local print firm, and had used them ever since he took over the stores twenty years ago. He would drop in on them on his way home.

"A technical label? No fancy graphics, just our logo, how to apply and how to clean up?"

"Sounds about it. But I would like you to think about labels generally. At some time I want to re-brand things." She smiled.

"Hardcastle and Mulligan?"

She came really close to him, as if to confide a great secret. He could feel the heat from her breath on his neck as she took him by the arm, and brought her lips close to his ear. As close as her amply proportioned body would allow.

"No Harry. Let's keep this a little secret between ourselves, but I intend to buy Hardcastle out before we begin to show too much profit. I was thinking of simply 'Mulligans', or perhaps 'Peckham Paints'. What do you think?"

Harry was not capable of speech for a while. As she hung on to his arm, and her perfume wafted up into his nostrils, his mind took him back to his late wife. His eyes misted over as she squeezed his arm, and turned him towards the door.

"Beg your pardon, Miss, I mean Tracey. But Mulligan's sounds more like the name for an Irish pub. I'd go for Peckham Paints if I was you."

She giggled. "Perhaps you're right Harry. Peckham Paints it is. But mum's the word for the moment. Eh?"

He nodded. Despite his advanced years, and his awareness that she spoke to all the men this way, he felt his heart rate increase as she escorted him to the door. He desperately tried to think of something to say to impress her.

"Perhaps we need to modernise our image. Meanwhile I'll speak to Potter and get the details from him. And I'll think of some alternative colour names, even if we don't decide on them yet. We can't use what he's calling them at the moment... And I'll get the printer to knock up some draft labels without a brand name."

Tracey giggled. "I don't know. I've a contact in a specialist clothing manufacturer who would be delighted with Potter's colour names. But I doubt there would be much profit in it. His garments are very small.'

She leaned slightly inward, pressing her body against his arm as she did so, and pecked Harry on the cheek as they reached the door.

"I know you'll sort it out. Let me know if Potter is a problem, but best not to mention names to him at this stage."

Harry left the office in a daze. He wanted to rub his cheek, but he also wanted to have a look in a mirror first to confirm he had not imagined it all.

He found Potter in the canteen. He was standing at the counter whilst the counter assistant, Edith, served him a rather generously portioned late lunch, with a double helping of gravy. A slim blonde girl he had not seen before stood behind her, stirring a bowl.

Harry joined the queue, and bought a mug of tea, before turning to look for where Potter had seated himself. He approached the table, and took a vacant seat opposite him. It took a while to get Potter's attention, as he sat and ate his meal, every so often looking up towards the counter and smiling, but eventually Harry got all the information he needed to get the labels printed.

"Why is the canteen so big?"

"What? Oh, I see. We used to have another product line, and twice as many staff, and the basement is just the space under the factory areas."

"So we could take a bit off the end there, below the loading bay?"

"I should think so. Why do you ask?"

"To be really efficient we need to use big sealed vats for paint production, but they are too heavy for a wooden floor, even if we could get them in. Besides, temperature control is easier in a cellar. If we built a goods lift to the loading bay, three men could make twenty times the paint, or more."

Harry nodded. Potter made sense. In fact it had been suggested before, but Herbert Strudwick had been adamant that they did no such thing. Harry had never understood it. Right after the war, when building materials were in short supply, they could have covered their costs on the reclaimed flooring and joists alone.

7. HIGH FINANCE, LOW TACTICS

On the last Thursday in July, Sebastian Hardcastle arrived at the factory for his monthly meeting, and to relieve them of his share of the takings. He was surprised, and somewhat annoyed, to see Henry Fothergill sitting in the boardroom with Tracey. He had come to enjoy his moments alone with her, and expressed his displeasure at the intrusion quite volubly.

"I didn't expect to see you here, Fothergill. So you've crept back after my nephew fired you. I wouldn't have thought you'd have wanted anything further to do with the place."

Tracey put down the sheet of paper she was reading, and smiled at Henry, before turning to face Hardcastle.

"I couldn't do without Henry. And he did not creep back. I had to use all of my powers of persuasion to entice him back to Gordon Road, including an increase in salary."

Hardcastle almost choked on the cup of tea he was holding. Increasing salary was not a tool in his armoury of staff management techniques. And he had a very good idea of what he thought constituted Tracey's powers of persuasion. Also, as she referred to him as Henry, he took a moment to realise she spoke of Fothergill. In the eleven years that Henry had worked for him, Hardcastle had never bothered to learn his first name.

"Well, perhaps you are getting your money's worth. The man looks decidedly weary."

Henry smiled sheepishly. He had not got a lot of sleep recently, but had no complaints. He was looking forward to the weekend, when his wife, Jane, had arranged for their children to visit an aunt, while she took him further into the realms of energetic bedroom role-play.

Tracey continued to face Hardcastle, and exaggerated her head movements to show she was inspecting him from head to toe.

"I see you are looking a little better today, Mr Hardcastle. I hope you are continuing to recover from your health issues... I asked Henry to join us, as we have now had time to fully evaluate the state of the company's finances. Were you aware that the factory is only leasehold? I'm afraid that failure to disclose that fact has a significant bearing on both the validity of our contract, and on my valuation for a 49% holding. Since the original structure was built in the late 1890s there is only 27 years left on the lease. A very different asset to what we were led to believe."

Tracey looked very solemn as she spoke. She waited with raised eyebrows when she finished speaking. Eventually Hardcastle broke the silence.

"You made a proposal, which I accepted. It was a straight business deal, young lady."

"It's not quite as simple as that," said Henry, as he took up the conversation that he and Tracey had anticipated when planning a strategy for the meeting. "You led Executive Services to believe that you owned the factory, whereas you merely leased it from a landlord. There were several witnesses to the discussions, including your nephew, whom I doubt would go out of his way to help you in his current situation."

Henry had guessed that, in addition to the charge of attempted murder, for which Ponsonby was currently detained in HMP Wormwood Scrubs, Ponsonby would also be aggrieved at the way Hardcastle had taken in his estranged wife and children, whilst insisting he be prosecuted and cutting him off. There was no love lost between the two, and Henry was on strong ground in supposing that the despicable Jason would take delight in giving evidence against his uncle.

Hardcastle's glare at Henry confirmed this, but Henry glared defiantly back. Eleven years of being treated as a dogsbody by Hardcastle had made him a most submissive person, but the few months of working for Tracey, and the past three weeks of re-kindled domestic passion, had turned him into a much more forceful character than Hardcastle was familiar with.

Tracey glanced at her watch. She had carefully choreographed the afternoon, and she anticipated being interrupted in two minutes.

"The problem is," she said slowly, continuing Henry's thread of discussion, "the law takes a very dim view of misrepresentation. I was talking about it only the other day to a friend who has investigated similar fraud cases. He says…"

Tracey broke off as she heard a knock on the boardroom door. Polly, who had been briefed on exactly how to interrupt them, waited a few moments after knocking, and then opened the door wide.

"I'm sorry to interrupt you, Miss Mulligan, but Mr Holmes is here and has asked if you could spare him a few minutes. He would wait, but he's got to get to the Magistrates' Court for a warrant before they close."

There standing behind Polly, but carefully positioned so that he was clearly seen by the room occupants, was the recently promoted Detective Sergeant Holmes.

"Why, Sergeant Holmes," said Henry loudly, "how nice to see you again so soon."

"Excuse me gentlemen," said Tracey, "I'll just be a few moments while I speak to the good sergeant. Please help yourselves to tea."

She got up and moved quickly, closing the door on her way out. As she left she wondered what Edith's tea would do to Hardcastle's recovering internal organs.

"That's the policeman who discovered my nephew was trying to poison me," said Hardcastle incredulously. "What's he doing here?"

Henry smiled, the sort of smile that a cat might smile when it had cornered a mouse.

"Yes. A razor-sharp mind, our Mr Holmes. Where would we, especially you, be without him...? I expect he wants to talk to Miss Mulligan about some documents she gave him to go over for her. I know he has been here a lot recently. Must make a change for him to be handling complicated fraud work. As a DC he was more used to dealing with gang crime. But of course, you know him, don't you. And no doubt know just how smart he can be."

Hardcastle went pale and thoughtful.

On the other side of the door, Tracey hugged Holmes, and led him to the far side of the room, well away from the possibility of being overheard. He picked up the half-drunk coffee cup that he had started while waiting for the precise time that Tracey had instructed Polly to interrupt them.

"I'll really owe you for this, Terry. I'll explain some other time. While you are here, I've got an uncle who is having trouble with noisy neighbours. Late loud parties and such like, and a pungent smell that's probably not Old Holborn. I wonder if you can do anything?"

He put down his cup, and got out his pocketbook to take a few details, while she went to Susan's desk and picked up a folder.

"I think you will find this interesting. It's a list of criminal connections of a used car dealer at Nunhead. It might be worth comparing his stock with descriptions from crimes involving cars. Also I think you might particularly like the reference to the Baptist Minister, who seems to borrow cars from him for late night outings rather than use his own vehicle: big cars with large boots, capable of carrying heavy loads. I think he may be quite adept at climbing the walls of buildings, especially country houses with lead roofs and lots of silver."

Holmes smiled. She had passed him several useful items recently, as she sought to close down her relationships with customers from her previous business, his superintendent being one of them.

Holmes's own relationship with her was entirely different: purely business, and definitely pure. Occasionally he wondered if he would prefer it to be more intimate, but he had an allegiance elsewhere; a demanding allegiance which ensured he was not starved of such company.

"I'll get Susan to see you out when you've finished your coffee. Give her your home address, and when we arrange the Christmas party I'll send you a pair of tickets."

She pecked him on the cheek, then turned and walked away. At the boardroom door she paused, and gave him a girlish wave before opening it, to give Hardcastle a reminder of the detective's presence. In the room Hardcastle and Henry were facing each other in silence.

"I'm sorry about that interruption, Mr Hardcastle. But it was most timely. Now where were we...? Oh, yes. Your valuation, before I bought into the company, is faulty. Also, based on current sales, this company is not worth the value of its debts.

If I go public with this knowledge then the impact on your other businesses would be devastating, but it would also almost certainly be the end of the factory, and my money. I really do not want to tarnish your business reputation so perhaps we can come to an agreement - say revalue my ownership as 75%, and accept a pro-rata amount for the remaining 25% of equity?"

Hardcastle stared at her. He mulled over the risks to his business of fighting her, but decided it was not worth the hassle, nor the risk to his other, more profitable, concerns that the publicity would inevitably bring. He nodded and sighed.

"All right, young lady. But make that cash, and a private treaty. I'll show it in my books as a tax loss, and we'll call it a deal."

Tracey could not believe her luck. She had expected him to haggle over percentages, but he had meekly accepted her base figure. She felt almost guilty as she made a mental note to talk to her favourite bank manager that evening. She picked up the phone in front of her.

"Mr Hardcastle is ready to leave. Can you get his chauffeur round to the front door?"

When Hardcastle had gone she jumped up, and hugged Henry.

"We did it!" she exclaimed exuberantly. "Now all we have to do is sort out Strudwick, and make a profit."

"And find the money to buy him out," said Henry as hugged her in return. He was becoming very tactile these days. Far from the cold fish he had been when they first met.

They were interrupted by the telephone.

"Miss Mulligan? Catherine Humber here. I'm ringing to warn you that my brother is intent on visiting the factory. I've tried to reason with him, but he seems obsessed. The doctors think he will be well enough to leave the hospice for a few hours next Monday."

8. GOOD EMPLOYEE RELATIONS

On the following Monday, Tracey Mulligan arrived early at the factory, long before any of her staff, and began a tour of inspection. She finished at the stores, and was having a quick look round when Reg came in.

"Hello, Miss."

"Now then, Piggy, there's no need to be formal when we are alone."

She made the words sound seductive, but Reg knew there was an invisible barrier there that would go up if he made a move in that direction.

"What can I do for you, Tracey?"

"We might get a visit from Herbert Strudwick. I don't want him to learn about the new product. Can you hide the paint?"

Reg thought for a while. The trial product was in a can about the same size as a tin of beans, whilst their French polish was stored in glass bottles at 24 to the box. The shiny stacks stood out immediately as you entered.

"I can stack a wall of empty polish cartons in front of those two shelves, and lock the door to the little store. It will make it look like very cramped in here though."

"That will have to do. I just can't take the risk of word getting back to Hardcastle before we complete the purchase of the factory."

Piggy frowned as he took in the implication of her words.

"I've just negotiated to buy Hardcastle out, and I believe that Strudwick knows him. If he got to hear that we had a new product line, he might have second thoughts about the deal."

Piggy stared, speechless for several minutes.

"So you'll be the sole owner?"

"Not yet. I've a friend who has put money into the business, and there's also the bank. It will take some time to pay back the bank."

"I could lend you some money if that would help," said Piggy thoughtfully.

"You?"

"Ernshaw left some money with me when he went to Spain. At the time he thought I was going to act as go-between between him and his gang. But I've not been approached by any of them since they arrested Bald Peter. Most of them are in prison... but I can't really put it in the building society, can I?"

"How much, Piggy?"

"About four-thousand pounds. I don't like keeping it at home."

Tracey gritted her teeth. It was exactly the same amount as the shortfall in how much Ernshaw had returned to her, when she threatened to expose him.

"Thank you, Piggy, that would be very helpful. I'll talk to Fothergill and see what the best way of absorbing it is. I can't just give you a receipt, can I?"

Piggy nodded. Since taking his job, he had learnt a lot about the way business relies on documents to track money, mainly while breaking into offices and copying those same documents. This reminded him of an earlier conversation.

"When do you want me to have a look at Strudwick's home?"

"We can leave that for a bit, and I'm not sure he even has a home now. In fact, Strudwick plans to come here today, so I might find another way of sorting him out."

Piggy let his mind wander into the realms of the various methods it was rumoured that Tracey had of sorting out men. He wouldn't have minded a bit of being sorted out himself.

Having completed her tour of the factory, Tracey was in the mood to waste a little time reminiscing. She and Piggy were sitting side by side, talking over amusing past events, when Harry arrived.

"Nice to see you back, fit and well, Harry. I'll leave Reg to bring you up to date. Incidentally if we do make a success of this new line I'd like you to stay on beyond Christmas. Have a chat with Henry Fothergill about it. I understand that deferring your pension can make a considerable increase when you do eventually draw it."

She stood, smoothed down her skirt, and left. Harry closed his eyes and took a deep breath through his nose, her perfume filling his nostrils and his mind. He was about to exhale, when she came back into the room.

"Sorry, I nearly forgot. Harry, I've got an aunt visiting from Cheshire next week. I'd planned to spend a few days showing her around, but this Strudwick business makes that impossible. Could you be a dear and do it for me: in the firm's time of course, and I'll give you a float to cover expenses. She arrives next Monday."

The door closed behind her, and Harry looked at Reg.

Reg burst out laughing.

"What's so funny?"

"Tracey Mulligan always gets what she wants, but this beats everything. You're to escort some old biddy round town for her. I never saw that in your job description. Still at least you'll see the sights at the company's expense."

Harry scowled as he took it all in. Then he nodded at the door.

"Reg, what exactly is your relationship with her?"

Reg sighed, looked at Harry for a while, and then stood up.

"Not what I could wish it to be, but it's a long story, and I'm not sure you'd believe half, but let's get a mug of tea and I'll tell you a bit about it."

In the canteen Reg got two teas and two slices of Bakewell tart. Mary smiled at him as he placed his order. Edith was in a funny mood, grunting in response to Harry's greeting, instead of her usual cheery reply.

Reg led Harry to a quiet corner, and they sat and sipped their tea warily. But, for the first time ever, the tea tasted pleasant. Reg looked up in surprise, and began his story. He started with Tracey getting him the job at the factory. He missed out the part about him being in prison, and concentrated on the bit about her persuading the Employment Office to only offer him as a candidate when the firm placed a vacancy with them.

Harry listened with widening eyes as Reg revealed that the reason Mabel had fallen on him and put him in hospital, was because Tracey coshed her from behind. He sat, mouth agape, as Reg told how he had broken into the factory to find information about the missing Sir Arthur. Finally when Reg revealed that it was him who had seen the rat poison and peppermint cordial Ponsonby had tried to poison his uncle with, Harry could maintain his silence no longer.

"Bugger me! And I thought you a puny little urchin, with a bland past. It looks like I really will have to watch myself with you around."

"Well that won't be long, will it? If you retire just after Christmas."

"I don't know Reg. These days it's more fun at work than at home on my own. Even being off sick for a week or so got boring. If staying on does make a difference to my pension then it would be worth it, if only to watch what you get up to."

The pair talked for some time, and Mary kept looking across. After a while she brought over two more mugs of tea. Harry looked in awe at Reg as she put the mugs down, and gave Reg a smile that suggested more than a casual acquaintance.

"Thanks, Mary. Did you make this?"

"Yes."

"It's different. Are you using a different brand?"

Mary laughed.

"No. Edith can't stand the smell of tea, so she throws a quarter pound packet in the urn without opening it. On a Monday afternoon she then dilutes it with boiling water, and on a Wednesday she throws in a second packet and tops it up with water now and again. Judging by the sludge I got out it must have been months since she last emptied the urn."

Harry looked at the mug in front of him, then across to where Edith stood behind the counter.

"But if you are now making the tea, why is she so grumpy today?"

"Alfred Potter never came in for his tea break. He always has a mug and a bacon roll... And a few minutes in the cold store with Edith."

Harry and Reg looked at each other.

"He was upstairs earlier this morning. They made 'gushing cream' and were planning to do a batch of 'tingling tangerine' before lunch. Perhaps they got pre-occupied. Or he might have had to go back to his shop to get something."

Mary looked blankly at Reg.

"It's a secret new product range. I'll explain this evening."

She picked up the empty mugs, and went back to the counter.

Harry looked at Reg.

"You and Mary, the new canteen assistant?"

"That's another story, but it will have to wait for another time. She's just lodging with me... For the moment anyway."

"You really are full of surprises. But we ought to get back to work. You nip up to the production area, and see what needs to come down. I'll meet you at the hoist."

Reg drained his mug. He waited for the expected stomach rumble, but it never came. Mary's tea had none of the purgative effect of Edith's.

Upstairs he started in the blue and white decked Millwall supporters' room, and worked his way along. In the Wolves room he found three men all stuck with their hands in a mixing bowl. He immediately knew which one was Potter, as two wore gold and black facemasks whilst the third man wore a plain white one. The white masked head started nodding frantically at him as he walked in. Reg walked over and lifted the mask.

"Help!"

"What's up?"

Potter glared across the workbench at the shorter of the two stirrers.

"He got the mixture wrong. He put in ounces when it should have been grams. We were doing an initial mix by hand, and it set."

Reg looked down at the bright orange mass in the bowl. Six hands disappeared into the solid rubber block.

"What can I do?"

"See that Stanley knife over there? Get it and cut away little bits, starting from the centre."

Reg did as asked, and sought access to the bowl. There was little space with the three men reaching across the bench from different sides, so Reg climbed onto the far end and walked along. Soon he was kneeling and cutting the block away, inch by inch until the rubber was weakened enough for Potter to free the remaining mass from the vat. The three men then walked sideways away from the bench to continue the process of breaking free.

"But why were all three of you stuck?"

"Because Malcolm and I were mixing the dry ingredients, and that twerp poured in twenty ounces of activator, instead of twenty grams!"

The twerp looked at Potter and began to protest. "But I tried to pull you out."

"Yes, by plunging your hands into the setting mixture!"

"How was I to know it would set like that?"

"Well, perhaps the mixture bubbling like a volcano, and the fact that neither of us could remove our hands by ourselves, might have been clues. None of the other mixes have done that have they?"

While this heated exchange continued, Potter managed to free one hand completely from the mass, albeit with numerous lumps still adhering. Potter had rather hairy arms and backs to his hands. The final clean-up was going to be painful. Reg could see that the verbal exchange was about to become less verbal, and more physical, so he retreated to the sanity of the stores.

"Did you find Potter?" Harry asked as Reg pushed the laden trolley into the store.

"Yes, he had got stuck into his work, and couldn't get away."

Reg had a fit of the giggles, and Harry looked quizzically at him.

"Sorry, Harry. You should have seen them. Masked up and joined at the wrist. I think Potter is having serious doubts about the team's ability to learn new skills."

"Let's hope he never has to work with the Millwall team then. It took Stanley Capes six months to get them to clock in and out properly. It was only when he drew blue and white lines on their buff time cards, and put 'home' and 'away' labels on the time clocks above the 'in' and 'out', that they began to get the idea. Even then there was always confusion on a Monday after a home win, and they will only stay late to work overtime if you call it injury time."

9. OLD CHICKENS COME HOME

The rest of the week passed in almost boring tranquillity. On Friday the whistle sent Reg scurrying home to the company of Mary. Working in the canteen she started, and finished, an hour earlier than the workforce. As he opened the front door he smelt the comforting aroma of dinner.

"Hi, I'm home," he called.

"We are in here, Reg," came the reply.

But it was not Mary's voice. It was an older, more familiar voice.

"Mum?"

"In the kitchen, Reg."

He charged into the kitchen. He was happy to see his mother, but at the back of his mind alarm bells began to ring. If she recognised Mary as Ernshaw's maid then there was bound to be trouble.

But in the kitchen the "we" did not include Mary. His mother was talking to a tall, thin, deeply suntanned man.

"This is Pepe. He is a friend who flew over with me for a few days."

Reg looked at the man, his mind starting to form a number of questions. Questions that he dared not ask while the man stood there. He also wondered where Mary was.

"I see you've had company while I've been away."

Reg thought for a moment, and then realised that Mary's few possessions were in his mother's bedroom.

"I can explain."

"No need to, Reg, I'm sure that Mabel has been looking after you."

'Mabel?' thought Reg. 'How can she possibly think the clothes scattered around could be Mabel's. They were about six sizes smaller.'

He smiled. "What's for dinner?"

"I don't know. The oven was on when we arrived. Perhaps Mabel has popped out to get something at the shops."

"It's not Mabel, Mum. Mabel is in Holloway, and not coming back. I've had a friend staying.'

"Do I know her?"

"I don't think so. Her name's Mary, and she came up from Devon a couple of months ago. She's a friend of Edith in the canteen at work."

His mother opened the oven, pulled a large Pyrex dish out and placed it on the hob. Her hitherto silent companion looked at it, and sniffed.

"Es Capporrones!"

"What?"

"Is Espanish. Beans and sausage and tomato. In my home town we call it the windy dish."

Reg's mother looked at her son. There was only one person she knew in England who could make such a meal. But as far as she knew she was dead, and rumour had it that Reg had been her killer.

"What's going on, Reg?"

"Honest Mum, it's just a friend. I expect it's a Devon recipe that is a bit like a Spanish one. My friend is a cook. She works at the factory. She tries out all sorts of meals at home that can be made on a canteen scale. I expect she made that for me to try, and then went out to her evening class."

Reg was clutching at straws, and suddenly realised that attack might be better than defence.

"What are you doing here, Mum? I thought you were in Spain with Big Ernie. When you didn't write I didn't know if you got married or not. Ernie said he was planning an August wedding."

"I'm, I'm just back to get a few things. Ernie is away at the moment."

"What do you mean, away? You were both away. Away in Spain."

"He's in Morocco."

"So you decided to come home for a visit. How long for?"

"He'll be in Morocco for quite some time."

"I meant, how long are you home for!"

"Just a few days, but there's no need to rush back. Ernie will be away for a while."

Reg frowned as his mother repeated the emphasis on how long her paramour would be absent. Then his suspicions got the better of him.

"Can you be more specific?"

"About five years."

"I take it that this is an enforced stay, rather than by choice."

"It wasn't his fault. He's too trusting. He brought in a shipment of hashish for an Arab friend, but it wasn't hashish, it was guns. The guards were waiting for him, and they sent him back to where the guns came from."

Reg looked at his mother in amazement. She seemed to have developed a very muddled sense of values since taking up with Ernshaw. And she still had not given him a clue about who her companion was.

"You two have my dinner. I've got to see a friend tonight anyway. Don't wait up."

He turned, and made it to the door before she could reply. Outside he scanned around in the hope of seeing Mary, but there was no sign of her. He walked down the stairs to the ground, and paused before setting off across the scrubby grass towards *The Squinting Badger*. As he passed the post office a slim figure stepped out of the doorway, and slipped her arm in his.

"Jeez, Piggy boy. That was a close one. I thought I was done for."

Reg turned to her. He had a million questions, but they could wait. He turned anxiously to check that they were out of sight of the flat.

"How did you get out?"

"I was putting some crumbs on the windowsill for that robin when I saw them get out of a taxi. You don't get many taxis round here. Minicabs, yes, but not black cabs. I grabbed my purse. and went up to the sixth floor. Then I waited until they went inside and scarpered. I would have stopped you on your way in, but I was in the phone box at the time."

"Who were you calling?" he asked. But before she could answer a dark blue J4 police van drove past, followed by a Hillman Hunter.

"I think the man with her is Ernshaw's Spanish number one henchman. With a bit of luck he will be in the cells soon. I know the Spanish police want him, and I think French police do as well."

Reg watched as Detective Sergeant Holmes, passing in the Hunter, gave them a wave and a grin, and then quickened his pace towards the pub.

Once safely tucked in a quiet corner of the public bar, they sat and talked for an hour or more, before deciding to make a move. It was clear that Mary could not come back to the flat, and neither of them had eaten. There was a glass cabinet of curled up sandwiches and pork pies on the bar to justify the pub's late supper licence, but Reg had never seen anyone buy anything from it. They headed towards Nunhead, and picked up Saveloys and chips along the road, to eat on the way. Half an hour later, full of stomach and greasy of finger, Reg pressed the doorbell of a little two bed terraced house behind Nunhead cemetery.

It took a long time before the door opened. A dishevelled Harry looked out into the gathering dusk at his visitors, and grinned foolishly.

"Hello, Harry. Can we come in? We're in a spot of trouble."

Reg expected Harry to immediately usher them in, but he hesitated.

"Is this a bad time?"

Harry wavered, and then stood back to admit them. As Piggy walked down the narrow passage towards the back parlour the unmistakable scent of *Evening in Paris* crept up his nose.

'No,' thought Reg. 'It can't be!' A vision of Harry and Tracey Mulligan flashed through his mind, but he dismissed it immediately as ludicrous.

As he entered the room a woman stood there, struggling to fasten a recalcitrant blouse button. Reg stared. She was in her early fifties, her blonde hair, lightly streaked with grey and her nails were painted a bright red. She grinned, and Reg tensed in anticipation of its familiar effect. There was no mistaking the family resemblance, and old biddy she most certainly was not!

"Hello, I'm Doreen. I think you may know my niece, Tracey."

Reg thrust forward a greasy hand, and she took it firmly. Mary followed him into the room, but Harry disappeared into the kitchen, leaving them to make their own introductions. He returned shortly after, with a tray of tea crockery and a slab of David Greig's Genoa cake.

"I see you've introduced yourselves. Doreen arrived early, and was getting under Tracey's feet a bit, so she's staying with me for a few days."

"Oh!" said Reg. "I was hoping that Mary could stay here for a bit. I didn't know you already had a guest. I'll have to think of somewhere else."

Harry looked embarrassed. He opened his mouth to speak, but Doreen got in first. She smiled at Mary, and took her by the arm reassuringly. Reg recognised that easy tactile way she forged links with strangers. He had seen it, and been subjected to it himself in the early days, as the persuasive Tracey bent him, and others, to her will.

"Of course you can stay. Harry will just have to put up with me all night instead of evenings only. I'll go and move my things. Is that okay, Harry?"

Reg's jaw dropped. Mary giggled, and quickly left to attend to a kettle that she had just heard click off the boil. Doreen swayed out of the room, with that combination of elegant deportment and sheer female magnetism that Reg and Harry were so familiar with in her niece, as she went upstairs to rearrange her alleged sleeping arrangements, and to give Harry time to get over his embarrassment.

Harry gave a sheepish grin, and dropped into an old armchair. He motioned to Reg to take another opposite him.

"What's the problem, Reg?"

"It's a long story."

"It always is with you, but I expect we've got time."

"You remember when PC Walker came, and arrested me on suspicion of murder?"

"How could I forget?"

"Well, Mary was the one I was supposed to have murdered."

"But I thought that was a Spanish maid named Maria, who worked for Ernshaw!"

"Yes, but her proper name is Mary. It was that detective, Mr Holmes, who set it all up, so that Big Ernie would think I'd done as he ordered, and she would be safe. We staged it all to convince Bald Peter."

"The one that they nicked for concealing a body?"

Reg nodded.

"The one that the Peckham Echo had a full page spread, with photos of the arrest, and the van spewing smoke out the back?"

Reg nodded again, and smiled as he thought of how thorough Holmes had been in setting up the arrest, with the press photographer friend of his following along behind him to accidentally stumble on the scene.

"Well, if it was not Mary who they found, who was it?"

"A leg of pork, and some butcher's bones."

Piggy then took some time to expand on this abbreviated tale, with Harry punctuating the narrative with a string of chuckles and giggles.

"You mean that he went to jail for transporting a leg of pork?"

"And torturing Sir Arthur Brain, and driving a stolen van... sorry three stolen vans welded together... and driving on several bank raids, and lorry hijacking. But the police did not have any evidence until he copped a plea and confessed to the lot, in exchange for the police dropping the murder charge."

"So why do you need Mary to stay here?"

"My mother's turned up from Spain, and she has a foreign looking man with her."

"And she would recognise Mary as Maria, and tell Ernshaw?"

"I don't know, but they both could. Mary looks very different with curly blonde hair, but if she stays in the flat long, Mum's bound to suspect. Besides, there are only two bedrooms."

"But I thought…"

"No. We're friends. Good friends, but we're not rushing anything."

At this inopportune moment, Doreen came back down, and sat on the arm of Harry's chair. He slipped an arm round her back to support her. She slapped it away playfully, as if to say, 'not in front of the children'. Clearly she and Harry had no qualms about rushing things. When she heard Doreen come down the stairs, Mary, who had been waiting in the kitchen to save any embarrassment, came in with a teapot and a bottle of milk.

"Any idea who your mother's companion is?" asked Harry.

"None, but Mary thinks he's a Spanish thug working for Ernshaw. I'll call Mr Holmes later and ask him."

Harry raised an eyebrow.

"Mary called the police. They were arriving just as we left."

Doreen who had heard little of the conversation frowned, and leant forward to pour the tea. Reg watched as the movement emphasised her figure, and he marvelled at just how closely she resembled her niece. Harry saw him watching her, and smiled.

They sat and talked until Harry started to yawn. Mary nudged Reg, and got up and walked him to the front door. In the relative dark of the passage she clasped his hand, and pulled him close. There they stood to say a long lingering goodnight. They were good friends, and slowly getting closer day by day.

10. NEVER A DULL MOMENT

When Reg got home, the flat was empty. The front door had a decidedly battered look, and he guessed that the men in blue had not bothered with the doorbell. He went in, and found their barely touched dinner in two bowls on the kitchen table. He tidied up as best he could, before going to bed.

He took a long time to fall asleep, but when he did he started to dream. It was a different dream to those he had experienced recently: most of which featured Mabel as King Kong to his Fay Wray. It was much less alarming, decidedly enjoyable. In it he was surrounded by a dozen or more attractive women, and was the centre of attention. One of the women, a particularly well developed lady, approached him, unbuttoning her blouse as she came.

At that point Reg was woken by sounds in the flat. Initially he considered hiding in the wardrobe, but then he heard a voice.

"Reg, are you still awake?"

"Yes, Mum."

"Can we talk? Are you alone?"

Reg shut his eyes, but the voluptuous 40DD who had been about to loom over him was gone. He got up, and put on a dressing gown.

"Yes, Mum. I'm alone," he said disappointedly.

"I'm afraid I'm going to have to make it a short visit. My friend has been arrested, and I'm not sure that they won't come after me too."

"Who, Mum?"

"The police. They came just after you went out, and took us away. They let me go, and I've been up The Arches on an errand, but I don't think it wise to stay there, or here."

"Who was that man with you?"

"Pepe? He works for Ernie. Ernie says he's a problem solver. I think he runs Ernie's import-export business as he's often away. But the police seemed to have mixed him up with a criminal. They said they were keeping him while an Interpol man comes over from Paris to interview him."

"So how long are you staying, Mum?"

"I'm taking the seven o'clock flight to Malaga. Are you keeping all right? Perhaps you could come out to see us sometime. Ernie has a lovely villa overlooking the sea, and a big hotel in the port. It's different out there. All very casual. He seems to have lots of staff in the hotel, but you can't be sure how many, as they all seem to walk round in bikinis. They are very attentive to the guests, especially the men. Come to think of it, almost all the guests are men. I suppose they are sailors waiting for new ships."

Reg smiled. His mother still hadn't cottoned on to the fact that it was a bordello.

"Have you seen Mrs Fisher, Mum?"

"Only the first few days. Then she went off somewhere. Might be Majorca, as Ernie sent her on his boat and it was not gone very long."

Reg nodded. He suspected it was probably a bit short of Majorca where Ernshaw had left her, probably in fairly deep water. He would have blamed her for having a son like Fingers, who turned grass on them.

"How are the plans going for the wedding?"

She looked at him, and sighed.

"There's a bit of a problem. Apparently you need a birth certificate, and Ernie only has a passport. Well three actually, but only one in his name. And that one would upset the Spanish authorities. I had no idea that international business was so complicated. Ernie tells me that Ernshaw is not a very nice word in Spanish, so he uses a different name. If we can't get married in our real names there don't seem much point in marrying under a false one. Besides, now I've got to wait for him to come back from Morocco."

"Five years?"

"No, Pepe says it will be much sooner than that. He came over with me to arrange Ernie's release. It's all a misunderstanding really. Pepe says that the man we gave a package to at Gatwick should get Ernie out in a week or so."

Reg sat and looked at his mother. How could she possibly believe that running guns instead of drugs was a misunderstanding? And her naivety about Ernshaw's business activities beggared belief.

"I'll be gone when you get up. I've booked a minicab for five o'clock. I'll write and let you know how things are when they settle down. Perhaps you would like to bring your friend Mary out for a visit. Ernie has lots of room, and there's always his hotel."

Reg went back to bed, hoping to renew his acquaintance with Miss 40DD, but sleep eluded him, and he was still awake when he heard his mother get up about four o'clock. He drifted off as he heard her close the front door, and did not open his eyes again until after nine o'clock.

Reg ran to the factory. There had been no time to shave or tidy himself, and he clocked in at 9:37. In the stores he found Harry humming to himself as he pasted labels on cartons.

"Hello, Reg. What kept you? Mary and I have been in for hours."

"My mother came back, but her companion is in Peckham Nick. Now she's gone back to Spain, and the flat is empty again."

Harry stopped pasting and looked up. He smelt strongly of aftershave, and faintly of *Evening in Paris*. There was a red patch on the side of his neck, just inside his collar. Like many youngsters, Reg had difficulty envisaging older people as being romantically active.

"I'm only in until lunch-time. Then I'm taking Doreen shopping in Oxford Street."

"Oh!"

"And Tracey stuck her head in a while ago. If you are not doing anything, would you like to join us for dinner in that Indian restaurant across from the cinema? About eight tonight."

"Us?"

"She said she might bring some friends of yours. By the way, she said not to bother about hiding the rubber paint tins. A Catherine something or other called her last night, to say that Herbert Strudwick was now in Lewisham Hospital with a broken hip."

"What?"

"Yes, apparently he fell over chasing a nurse in the sluice room. They are talking of putting a pin in his leg."

"Shame they don't slice his goolies off while they are about it. Speaking of which I was a bit surprised to see Tracey's aunt last night."

Harry blushed.

"It's funny Reg. I never thought I'd look at another woman after my Lizzie, but somehow it all seemed so natural. I woke in the middle of the night with an arm across me and that perfume... Just for a minute I thought... Well, you know."

He drifted off dreamily to gaze out of the obscure glass of the window for a while, before shaking his head and picking up the paste brush.

"You don't think Tracey put her up to it, to make you stay on, do you?"

Harry burst into laughter.

"I doubt I'm worth the effort, and she did put in a lot of effort!"

He continued to laugh for some time until tears ran down his cheeks. Then he pulled out what Reg assumed was a handkerchief from his pocket, and mopped his face.

"Harry?"

"Yes?"

"Since when did Janet Reger make handkerchiefs?"

Harry stretched out two corners of the cloth in his hand, revealing the briefest of ladies' briefs, then quickly crumpled it up and stuffed it back in his pocket.

"Oops! Wrong drawer!"

At twelve o'clock the door opened, and the lovely Tracey came in accompanied by the equally lovely, if slightly faded, Doreen. Harry hung up his warehouse coat, and put on a rather loud check sports jacket. Doreen slipped an arm in his, and the pair went off. Tracey watched them go, then turned to Reg.

"Clock Harry out when you go home, Reg. He's told you about dinner tonight?"

Reg nodded, and watched as she turned and wiggled out of the room. He wondered if she ever had any real feelings for a man herself, or if something in her past had put her off for life. Her aunt seemed to have taken to Harry in a big way. Reg shook his head as if the action would make thought clearer. He was used to older people lapsing into a sort of slow-motion torpor, not dating and mating. He combed his hair, and made his way to the canteen. Since Mary had joined the staff the menu had become more interesting, and the canteen more crowded at lunchtime.

Mary was too busy to say much as he queued at the counter, and in any case there were many ears about. But she smiled, and slipped an extra sausage on his plate under the cabbage. He found a table, and sat to eat his breakfast come lunch. As he dissected his second banger, Alfred Potter plonked a tray down opposite him, and sat down.

"I'd be better off training monkeys, like Brooke Bond do," he said. "I thought I'd let them make a batch of Seductive Green on their own this morning, and they've only gone and done exactly what they did yesterday."

"What? Got stuck?"

"Yes."

"How long did it take to free them?"

"What do you mean 'did it take'? I've left them up there. Giving them time to reflect on their mistake."

Reg looked at the man as he tucked in to an oversized soup course, with an extra-large bacon pudding to follow, and spotted dick to finish. He felt less guilty about his free sausage as he assessed the mound that Edith had served Potter: it was clearly not going to be a quick meal break. He was going to be there for at least half an hour. More if he had coffee afterwards, and judging by the way he was slowly supping his soup he was clearly in no mood to hurry his return. Reg made a mental note to avoid the Wolves' room that afternoon, and settled back to his own, single course, meal.

He was finishing the third sausage when a commotion over by the stairwell took his attention. Two masked men were walking crablike down the stairs, appearing to carry a large stainless steel bowl between them, yet Reg could not see any hands holding the outside of the bowl.

He nodded to Potter, and the man turned to see what all the noise was about, before pushing his empty soup bowl to one side. Potter then wiped his moustache on a serviette, and hunched forward to start on his bacon pudding.

Reg hastened to finish, and made his excuses to leave. As he did so, the gold and black masked, two-headed, four-legged monster spotted the hunched figure, and started to scuttle its way through the crowded canteen toward his table. Despite the masks, the noise level was quite loud, and the language used as they pushed their way forward was as colourful as the masks themselves. They arrived at the table, and thumped their load down with a bang.

Potter stopped eating, and looked at the bowl. He looked in silence for some time before tilting his head up towards the two men.

"Not bad. But it should be a little paler than that. It's called Seductive Green, not Emerald Green. Try a gram less blue, and a gram more yellow next time."

And then he returned his attention to his meal.

The monster stood stunned for a moment, and then both heads simultaneously emitted a roar as they raised the bowl above Potter's head. The vessel was already beginning its downward descent when a white aproned blur pushed the men sideways, so that the missile smashed the empty soup bowl instead of Potter's skull. The momentum of the push rolled both men to the ground, and there they lay as an enraged Edith stood over them, holding two heavy wooden spoons aloft ready to strike.

Potter paused from his meal for a second time, and again looked up.

"Thank you, Edith. That was most thoughtful. You've not forgotten our arrangements for this evening have you? Eight o'clock outside *The Star of the East.*"

He smiled at her. Then, as if the incident had been an insignificant distraction, he dropped his head back to his lunch, and continued to tackle the bacon pudding. The event seemed to have no more importance to him than a passing cloud on a sunny day. Edith prodded the prone pair in the ribs in an effort to encourage them to their feet, and then shepherded them towards the stairs. Any attempts to remain were thwarted by judicious application of the wooden spoons.

Back in the stores, Reg sat for a few minutes reading Harry's *Daily Sketch,* before picking up the telephone and dialling the CID office at Peckham. He eventually reached DS Holmes, and told him what his mother had said about Mrs Fisher. Holmes, in return, told him not to worry about Ernshaw's thug, Pepe. He was currently on his way to Marseilles under an escort of two gendarmes.

As a relieved Reg put the phone down, Holmes was reaching for his expenses form. In a neat hand he added an entry for refreshments for an informant whilst receiving information about a missing person. He then made a diary entry to pass on the information to Fingers Fisher, when he next met him. He was not so much thinking of putting him on guard, as expecting the man to remember further reasons why the police would want to talk to Ernshaw and his gang.

Fingers was very fond of his mother, and his first criminal record had been an arrest while stealing flowers on Mother's Day.

Holmes' lady-friend, Milly, was staying with him for a while. He would take her for a day out to Brighton, and see Fisher at the same time. Fingers was currently employed at the Police Nursing Home in Hove, as a cleaner under the name of George Green. He gave out monthly titbits of information in return for being anonymously lodged fifty miles from home, in a building full of police officers.

Holmes reached for his mileage claim form, before getting up to go and update Superintendent Hackworth.

11. LOVE IS IN THE AIR

Mary waited in the stores for Reg to finish work. She sat in Harry's chair watching him as he labelled and packed cartons, occasionally glancing at Harry's discarded Daily Sketch, but mainly following Reg about with her eyes. She had been trained from birth, by her mother, not to trust men, but in the past few months she had grown very fond of Reg. When she first met him, she viewed him as a hapless bit of life's flotsam, drifting about at the beck and call of others. But over time he had started to put down roots, and more particularly, distance himself from those elements of his past that his parole officer would consider undesirable.

His part in separating her from the clutches of her evil boss, Ernshaw, was something that would earn him her undying gratitude. Yet it was also that action that caused confusion in Mary's mind. Was this feeling for him love or gratitude? She really could not be sure. She had no reference point to compare her feelings with. So far she had expressed herself in the only way she knew how, as cook and housekeeper looking after him in the absence of his mother. But she knew that sooner or later that relationship would have to evolve, and she had no idea how, or when that would be.

Reg stopped work as the whistle blew, hung up his warehouse coat, and changed into his outdoor shoes. Recently he had taken to wearing a pair of Dunlop Green Flash tennis shoes in the factory as he found the dust meant he was otherwise constantly cleaning his outdoor wear. Lately, he had grown a bit fussy about his appearance, and the results showed. Mary shyly took his hand as they walked to the time clock in the cloakroom to mark the end of his day's toil, and Harry's fictitious exit from the building.

They walked home hand-in-hand chatting about trivia as they went. One should not read too much into their held hands. It meant no more than that they were friends with common interests and common intent: like two small children in a playground.

As they walked, neither wanted to talk about what they really wanted to know, in case they got the wrong answers to their questions. At home, after making a pot of tea, Reg sat watching Pinky and Perky while she had a bath. DS Holmes had quietly returned most of her clothes that had been used in his charade, as evidence of her death, to extract a confession from Bald Peter. But they seemed to belong to a different person, and she rarely wore them now.

Tonight she came out of the bathroom in a cotton print shift that she had bought in Jones & Higgins. Over her arm she had a long, belted cardigan. Her appearance was a marked contrast to the slacks and soft tops she generally now wore. It banished any hint of her usual tomboyish appearance.

Reg was spellbound. Like her he had been struggling to define his feelings and there, with the weak sunlight struggling through the grimy window behind her, he suddenly knew what they were.

"Gosh. You look lovely!"

She curtseyed, and smiled.

"Oh, thank you, kind sir."

Then, after a moment's thought about how things could possibly develop if they stayed in, she added, "Do we really have to go out tonight?"

Reg continued to gaze at her, and then finally stood up.

"I think we ought. Besides it will be nice to be with friends that we both know, and I don't think we will be out too late."

Reg and Mary were a little early arriving at the Indian restaurant, and they hung around outside reading the menu on display in the window.

The proprietress, Sharon, saw them, and her instinct was to go out and cajole potential customers in, but she looked at the clock, and guessed they were part of the large party booked for eight o'clock. She pushed her heavy bangles further up her arm, before returning to her task of slicing lemons. Soon after she saw an older man and woman join them on the pavement.

"Hello, Harry. Spent all your money?"

Harry smiled.

"No, lad. Doreen here was window-shopping. Seems there's nothing up West that she can't get in Chester for less. But it was worth getting sore feet just to confirm it."

Doreen smiled at Reg, and Mary squeezed his hand to remind him that she was there. As they stood waiting, Henry Fothergill drew up, and helped his wife, Jane, from their car.

Reg and Harry rarely spoke to Henry, although Henry and Mary often exchanged pleasantries at the canteen counter. They struggled to make small talk. All of them were relieved when Tracey arrived in a black cab: all except Jane Fothergill, that was!

A Hillman Hunter parked across the road. Mary, recognising the dark blue car with its distinctive two aerials on the front nearside and rear offside wings, turned to see who got out of it. Then dashed across the road.

"Milly, I didn't expect to see you."

The two women hugged each other, and came back towards the restaurant arm in arm.

"I've let the cottage for a few weeks. I'm staying with Terry."

Mary dragged her friend round the small group, introducing her to Tracey, Doreen and Harry. Tracey flashed her a smile, then turned to DS Holmes, who was following behind Milly.

"This is unexpected, Terry. You are both welcome to join us. I'm just waiting for one other, and I think you know him."

As she spoke, John Dillon came round the corner.

"Ah, here he is. Come on then, let's go in."

She reached for the door, but it opened inwards, pulled by a thickset waiter who bowed slightly to the party. He took Doreen and Tracey's jackets in white-gloved hands, and then ushered them to an alcove, with a reserved sign on the table. He frowned as he counted two more people than chairs.

"I'm sorry, we seem to have grown to ten. Can you squeeze us in elsewhere?"

Charlie, known locally as Ahmed, smiled and motioned towards a large oval table. It was less private than the alcove, but considerably less cramped. He disappeared into the kitchen, to return with a set of 'specials' cards to supplement the menus on the table.

He stood expectantly as some browsed the wine list, but Tracey was ahead of them.

"Two carafes of house red, and two of white, please."

As they waited for the wine to arrive, they indulged in small talk. Both Tracey and Reg spotted Alfred Potter and Edith arrive and slip into a dimly lit alcove at the far end of the room. Tracey called back the retreating Charlie.

"Ahmed, please send a carafe of the house wine to that alcove over there, with my compliments."

Tracey smiled as she spoke, and Charlie nodded. He headed back to the kitchen to check on the bottle of industrial alcohol that was an essential ingredient of the house wine.

"Bah gumb, Christos. It's gonna be a busy night. Yon blonde tart has already ordered five of the house wine. I'd better give Sandra a ring, to see if she can pop along to the still."

"Is alright, init Charlie. I've got a jerry can of it in the van: in case I run out of petrol. Can you chop some of those beans while you're here?"

Charlie took off the gloves that Sharon insisted he wore in the dining room, and grabbed a knife. A duffle bag of six-foot long runner beans hung from a hat stand. Charlie pulled a few out. As he de-stringed and chopped the monsters, Christos was slicing blue potatoes and dropping them in a pot of curry sauce.

"Today's special, init. Chicken Biriyani," he said as he reached for the bowl of soya chunks soaking in chicken Oxo.

"We've got a new research contract at the college. Frost resistant tomatoes. So far they've all been brown and black striped with purple flesh. I'll have a word with the prof, and see what he wants for them. But that's the last of those potatoes. The latest test batches have all turned out creamy coloured."

Christos, and his wife Sharon, had been running the restaurant for ten years. Much of their produce came from the experimental programme at the agricultural college, as did their staff. Christos was particularly proud of the house wine. It consisted of a base of grape juice fortified by alcohol. The alcohol came from a still used to manufacture tractor fuel from sugar beet waste. A special, more expensive, sparkling version included a spoonful of Andrews Liver Salts to give it the required fizz, but that was strictly limited. Limited by the availability of the half dozen used champagne bottles, and Charlie's time to spend forcing the corks in and binding them there with thirty-amp fuse wire.

Charlie was currently awaiting the results of his degree dissertation on artificial insemination in beef cattle. It when Sharon became aware of Charlie's specialist subject that she had insisted he wore the white gloves, despite his insistence that most of his studies were theoretical, and that he wore rubber gloves on the few occasions when he was required to assist with the practical side of the work.

He would soon be heading back to the family farm outside Ripon in Yorkshire. He planned to take a holiday, and a crew-cut to shear off the black dyed hair, before he returned to the bosom of his family in his natural blond state. Christos and Sharon would miss their star waiter, but were training a first year student, Aiden, to take his place. Given Aiden's heavy Geordie accent and vocabulary, it was likely to be a long training period before he could pass as an authentic Indian waiter. Meanwhile Aiden helped in the kitchen, and silently served dishes to large groups in the company of Charlie: the original dumb waiter!

The only authentic Indian ingredients in the place were the ten-pound drums of curry powder which Christos got from a contact at Heathrow, and the occasional sari from Ealing Broadway when Sharon could not find suitable curtain material roll-ends in East Lane market. Even the exotic jewel encrusted 'leather' sandals she wore were flip-flops, painted with brown and gold lacquer, and adorned with transparent Pop-It beads. She was especially pleased with her set of silver Indian bangles, consisting of two chromed compression and three oil retention piston rings from a Hillman Minx.

In the dining room the talk had turned to the menu, and Sharon hovered to advise on some dishes before Charlie returned with the wine. She then glided gracefully away whilst he took their order. He helpfully suggested garlic naan and bahji as accompaniments.

Christos had some football-sized onions, and dry pittas that were past their best, both of which needed to be consumed before further deterioration made their presence in the hot kitchen too undesirable.

Having ordered, Tracey tapped on the table with a spoon to get everybody's attention.

"I had a special reason for calling you all together tonight. Most of you here have been instrumental in me successfully achieving the career that I have dreamed of since my first day at university, and for that I thank you. It is fortuitous that Terry Holmes and his good lady, Milly, have joined us, as he had no small part in securing our future. Each of you knows how you have helped me, and I intend to repay you all as best I can. But I also have another reason to celebrate tonight... John and I are to be married."

John Dillon smiled as she finished speaking, but all others just sat and stared: glasses en route to mouths hovered in mid-air, napkins hung above laps and faces struggled to find appropriate expressions. Neither Reg or Holmes, both of whom had regular contact with Dillon, had any inkling of this relationship between Tracey and the former policeman. Holmes knew that after the Goose Green poisoning, Dillon had become so work obsessed that it had destroyed his marriage, but assumed he was now resigned to a life of bachelorhood. Tracey spread her affections so widely throughout the male population that no one could envisage her devoted to just one man.

"When's the happy day?" asked Milly, who knew less of Tracey than all others at the table.

"I'm afraid that it won't be for a while yet. We've a few financial and legal things to sort out first."

Tracey grinned at Dillon as she finished speaking. She had to disentangle herself from the local bank manager, and close down her other business before the happy day. Dillon had to obtain a divorce from his wife, who was last heard of working as a hairdresser on a cruise liner.

Harry glanced at Reg. Since that young man had become his assistant, his whole world had turned upside down. He had spent thirty-eight boring years as a storeman, yet now both work and social life had been enlivened, with rarely a dull moment at either. He squeezed Doreen's hand, hoping he had the energy to see him through the night.

But Harry had confidence. He was now taking treble daily doses of Phyllosan tonic, in the hope that it lived up to its advertising slogan of 'Fortifies the over-forties'. His self-calculated dosage was based on an extra spoonful per decade over the recommendation. So far he had no cause to complain about its efficacy, and Doreen had every reason to approve of his self-medication.

As the dishes arrived, and the wine began to flow, they all settled to the serious business of enjoying themselves. Jane Fothergill had seemed a little tense when she arrived, but relaxed considerably after Tracey's announcement. Christos was his usual inventive self and supplied a wide range of colours and textures to sit in the dishes to tempt them, despite the very limited and somewhat odd ingredients he had used.

As with any group where most work together, the talk eventually got round to the factory, and the prospects for the future.

"Tonight is not the time for shop talk, but I will say that things now look better than they have for a long time." It was Henry who spoke, and Jane who whispered in his ear after he did. He tittered as he took in the full implication of the promise she had just made. Most definitely things looked better for him. He wondered if he should have a word with Harry, in case the man had any secrets to sustain him in his domestic activities. Harry certainly looked well for someone who would soon take possession of a pension book, and had recently taken up possession of the voluptuous Doreen.

At about ten o'clock, Potter and Edith slipped away from the restaurant, hand in hand. As they left it seemed to anyone watching that Edith was dragging Potter along at an indecent speed.

Harry again went to squeeze Doreen's hand, but found she had already sought his knee, and was slowly moving bodywards.

Mary, who had been talking to Milly, turned to Reg.

"Milly says that the cottage is let until the end of the month, but if we're prepared to tidy the garden and wanted to go down there after that for a week, she would be happy to have an excuse to stay on here a bit longer."

Reg looked from Mary to Milly, and back, before replying.

"Yes, I'd like that very much. But I'll have to check if Harry has any holiday plans first."

They both looked for Harry, but he was not there, neither was Doreen. Ten minutes later, the pair emerged from the facilities at the back of the restaurant. Doreen appeared to be freshly made up, and Harry had a lipstick-smeared collar which told the world the reason why she needed a fresh application of Yardley Holly Red.

"I think it's time we all went home, before it's too late," said Mary.

"Maybe it already is," replied Reg with a grin, as he glanced round the table at the various couples.

Shortly afterwards the party broke up. Tracey called for the bill, but Henry said something to her about tax, and took out a company cheque book. She nodded her agreement.

Sharon looked up from behind the bar, and scowled. She preferred to deal in cash.

12. IMPROPER PROPERTY

It was several days before Henry Fothergill got back to Tracey with his findings about the ownership of the factory. Herbert Strudwick had not been totally honest in his assertion that the factory was leased from him. The eight houses that made up the middle of the factory were freehold in the company name, but the rest were leasehold, with a William Strudwick holding the freehold of a block of five and Herbert Strudwick being the freeholder of the remaining properties.

Henry assumed that in the early days, Herbert had used company money to acquire property, but when he had amassed some personal wealth he had started to use the device of buying the property himself, and selling a lease to his own company at a higher price. It was not an uncommon ploy, designed to provide an instant cash sum, and a small on-going income when one calls a halt to their working life, and sells the business. Henry had no idea who William Strudwick was. His address on the documents was shown as a house in Gordon Road, one that was a part of the factory.

He had phoned Lionel Dee, who had been the accountant for the original company, but Lionel could not give him any immediate information; it all happened before he was engaged by the company. Lionel suggested that they contact Catherine Humber, nee Strudwick, to see if she could shed any light on the matter.

Henry briefed Tracey, and suggested that perhaps they consider changes to only the parts of the building that were freehold: but that was not a practical approach. Besides, Tracey was curious. She phoned Catherine at Strudwick & Wouters, and invited her to dinner.

To make the evening a social event rather than a blatant information gathering exercise, Tracey invited a number of other dinner guests. Of these only John Dillon, and her aunt Doreen, had ever been to her home before.

Harry Derry had grandiose preconceptions about where their flamboyant boss would live, and first impressions came as a bit of a letdown. He stood and pressed the doorbell on an unobtrusive, traffic stained, street door, in the flank wall of a short modern parade of shops. Whilst waiting for a response, he espied a familiar figure with a distinctive gait approach, arm in arm with a woman he recognised as Catherine Strudwick.

"Hello Harry, not seen you for a while. What are you doing here?" boomed Sam Humber.

"Same as you, you old rascal: escorting a lady."

"Imaginary lady, unlike my lady wife here?" asked Sam, as he looked around theatrically for a second person.

"She's the boss's aunt. She should be here already... Did you say wife?"

"Certainly!" said Sam, adopting a more formal tone, "May I present Mrs Catherine Humber... Better known to you as Catherine Strudwick."

Sam chuckled and thrust forward a hand, but Catherine stepped closer, and bestowed upon him a kiss on each cheek. Recovering his composure after this unexpected show of affection, Harry returned his gaze to inspect his much altered old friend. He looked nothing like the bearded, unkempt character that had worked as a porter in the old days when Herbert Strudwick was in charge of the factory. He was clean-shaven, smelling of aftershave, and neatly dressed in sharply pressed cavalry twill slacks and sports jacket. Even the shoe on his artificial left foot was the same colour and pattern as the right one: a rare event in the old days!

A buzzing sound announced that the door could be pushed open, so the three of them entered a dark, narrow lobby with a flight of bare concrete stairs facing them. Harry took the lead, with Catherine following and Sam at the rear, like a team of climbers approaching an uncharted steep face.

As they neared the top a door opened ahead of them, bathing the stairwell in light, and releasing a subtle hint of the nature of the impending dinner. A bare-footed Tracey, casually dressed in crimplene flared trousers and a flowery tabard over a short-sleeved lace top, stepped into the doorway and grinned.

"All together? No need to keep dinner waiting then. Harry, I think you know everybody. Can you make a few introductions while I finish in the kitchen? John will get you a drink."

Harry scanned the huge lounge. He found John Dillon and Doreen at the far side, and beckoned Catherine and Sam towards them.

The décor and condition of the flat was greatly at odds with its shabby entrance. It had an expensive oriental feel, and was considerably larger than he had expected from outside. It ran the width of several of the shops below, with a large roof garden at the rear. Inside rich, intricately patterned rugs were strategically placed on deeply polished woodblock floors, lit by gold light fittings with pearl shades. Rosewood furniture stood against a muted cream background of patterned flock wallpaper, and huge gilt mirrors reflected the light, creating the illusion that the room was even larger than it was. It put Harry in mind of a picture he had once seen of the Palace at Versailles.

Conversation over dinner was dominated by Harry and Sam catching up on a year's work gossip, with Tracey and Catherine making polite incursions during the infrequent pauses. Doreen sat quietly beside Harry, and said little. Although a relative of Tracey she was the odd one out, with few shared experiences except her recent involvement with Harry.

With all else dispatched, John Dillon went to the kitchen to make a pot of coffee, and to arrange a salver of almond macaroons, whilst the remaining diners moved to a pair of low backed settees. Soon the smell of Moka D'Or, from the Drury Coffee Company under the arches at Waterloo Station, fought to compete with *Evening in Paris* and Sam's aftershave in the noses of those assembled. Harry watched John, as he moved about with the precise action of one who was very familiar with his surroundings.

Over coffee, Tracey finally managed to broach the subject for which she had arranged the evening.

"By the way, Catherine, I've had Henry Fothergill look into the status of the factory. It's rather complicated as some parts are freehold, and the rest leasehold."

"News to me," replied Catherine as she reached for another macaroon. "Whenever Herbert wanted to expand, he asked the family to buy shares, and then claimed to add another property to the site. He always told us he had bought them freehold."

"He might have personally bought the freehold, but he then sold the company a lease. There is another name on some of the documents. Who is William Strudwick?"

As Tracey asked the question, all eyes turned to Catherine. She took some time before answering.

"Never heard of anyone of that name... Wait, we had a great uncle Bill, but he lived in Rhodesia. Don't suppose it was him, though."

Catherine frowned after speaking, and contemplated the now half-eaten macaroon. There was a long silence before she looked up, and gave a faint smile.

"As a small boy, Herbert had an imaginary friend called William."

Simultaneously Harry and Sam spoke. "What?"

"Yes, our parents even let him have an extra-large bedroom, because he claimed that he shared it with William. And I seem to remember when he was a teenager an enquiry agent called at the house, looking for a William Strudwick. Something to do with a paternity suit, I believe."

"You mean that not only has he used a false name in business, but also has a child somewhere?"

"Oh, At least one," replied Catherine, in a rather commonplace manner. "For the few months he was at art college, you sometimes couldn't get in the front door for weeping young women. He was just as bad as a young man, running the factory, except I think he had an arrangement with a struck-off doctor to solve problems, if you know what I mean. It didn't do to ask too many questions."

Tracey took a gulp of coffee, and sat back, deep in thought. "So, for part of the factory we might have a non-existent landlord?"

Simultaneously the six of them lifted their coffee cups and drank. Then, with the china safely back on little cork-backed drinks coasters, depicting scenes from a Dickensian London, they sank back to absorb both the fluid and the information.

"What could be gained by using a false name to buy his own factory?" asked Sam to nobody in particular.

"I suspect it was about tax. Two persons, two personal allowances, and a very convenient alias for less than legal dealings. You've got to remember that there was a top income tax rate called supertax. Nineteen and six in the pound."

Catherine eyed the last macaroon as she spoke, and after a decent interval with no other claimants, took possession of it. John Dillon had been silent for most of the evening, with only the occasional short reply to direct questions, but now he coughed to draw attention to himself.

"If I remember rightly there was also a legal requirement, in the 1948 Companies Act, for a private limited company to have at least two directors, and a named company secretary. Who were the original directors of Strudwick's?"

"Just Herbert!" mumbled Catherine as she finished the macaroon. "But come to think about it, he never would let anybody see the company register, and we never had a named company secretary until he appointed Lionel Dee in the late fifties. We were all happy as shareholders, as long as our dividends were one percent more than the building society. In most years they were well above it. So, what with the monthly meal tokens in the canteen, and the annual dinner, no-one bothered to ask."

"But you must have had the accounts audited."

"Herbert handled that. But we never saw raw documents, only a summary that he wrote for the AGM. I had a sneaking suspicion that some transactions did not go through the books. He dealt with a number of special customers himself. Mostly little furniture factories. You know the sort: make reproduction antiques, complete with dummy woodworm holes. And then pass some off as genuine."

"So you think he might have been fiddling the books?" asked John Dillon, in a tone that would not have been out of place in the interview rooms of his former occupation.

"Well, some things did not quite add up. One example was the year when dividends were reasonable, but he bought his new house and that big Jaguar without selling his old home. He just sometimes seemed to have more money than the annual financial summary could account for."

Tracey shook her head. The evening had been a success in getting answers to the questions she knew to ask, bit it had created more questions.

Sam, who had been sitting quietly, now he gave a little cough.

"Has anyone looked in the Anderson?"

"The what?" asked Tracey and John simultaneously.

"The Anderson shelter. Originally there were bomb shelters in several of the back gardens. One was bigger than the rest and there was a tunnel knocked through from the basement for shift workers. When some of the poor devils were bombed out they bunked down in the shelter and the tunnel. It was where that thick wall in the canteen is now. One year we came back from the annual shutdown, and found the tunnel bricked up. Before that it was used to store sacks of shellac and boxes of stuff that Herbert Strudwick said was just junk. When I joined the firm there was a rumour that Herbert was involved in the black-market."

13. CURIOSITY

Tracey and Henry stood staring at the canteen wall. A section about eight feet wide was of a different brick to everywhere else, and the mortaring looked decidedly amateurish.

Harry Derry walked past, and glanced at what was holding their interest. He paused beside them.

"That's the spot where Herbert Strudwick always sat to eat his lunch. I always thought it was so he could watch Big Alice on the canteen staff lean forward over the counter to serve customers. Boy, that was a sight for sore eyes. But now I look at it, this is where the entrance tunnel to the Anderson was."

Henry nodded and pointed at the brickwork.

"It would be the ideal location for a new access to the loading dock if we moved paint production down here. Firstly we would need to open the area up to get big vats in, and then put in a goods lift to the loading bay. But it is right in the middle of a block that is leasehold."

Harry looked around, and pointed towards the end of the canteen before replying. "This must be where Strudwick started. His first house purchases were along there. I remember neighbours that side kicking up a fuss about the smell and noise. What with the wind being mostly from the south-west, they got it worse than the other side. And there was a right set to one day. A big bloke accused Strudwick of getting up to mischief with his daughter."

"Another little Strudwick somewhere?"

"Don't know anything about that. The Old Man probably bought his way out of trouble, one way or the other. Never saw the bloke again. I expect he took the money, and moved away. A lot of the houses were rented, and once someone moved out, nobody wanted to move in next to the factory. Herbert would leave it six months or so and then approach the landlord with an offer. But some would just disappear, without even taking their furniture, so we had to clear the houses as he bought them."

Tracey and Henry exchanged glances.

"We need a big hammer!" said Henry quietly as he envisaged all sorts of horrors hidden behind the bricks.

"I've got one at home," said Harry, "and some chisels. We had a coal bunker which I knocked down to extend the kitchen."

*****

On Thursday evening, a little group assembled in the canteen and cleared a space in front of the wall. Harry Derry seemed to know what he was doing, and had organised torches, brooms, buckets and dustpans for the others while he stood, mason's chisel and club hammer in hand, looking for a weak point in the wall.

"Is that hammer the right one?" asked an anxious Henry Fothergill as he spied a much heavier sledgehammer leaning against the wall a little way off. Harry grinned, as he waved his hammer in Henry's direction.

"Got to start small. No idea what's behind this until we open it up a bit."

He found the spot he was looking for and put the chisel to the mortar and tapped it. A few particles of crumbly mortar fell at his feet. He moved the chisel slightly and tapped again. Harry carried on like this for several minutes, working his way round the outline of a single brick, then he stood back a little way and hit the brick square in the middle. It cracked and half a brick disappeared into the void beyond with a dull thump. A few more blows and the remainder of the brick followed its other half.

Harry reached for a torch and shone it into the hole. Beyond was a long space with shelving and packing cases either side of a clear gangway. Harry attacked the brick above the hole and it came away with a few blows.

"Let me take a turn," said Henry.

Harry handed Henry a wide flat chisel.

"Hit the mortar of the partly free bricks either side, but don't go more than four bricks wide or you might bring the lot down."

Harry watched Henry for a while, then walked along to the canteen counter where Tracey had provided a tray of sandwiches and flasks of tea. He made his selection, and walked back to where Henry, Tracey and Reg stood. Henry removed bricks from three courses down from the original hole. The view inside the hole was becoming obscured by a cloud of brick dust. There was an odd smell which none of them could place: almost as if someone was eating sweets. No; not sweets, marzipan!

Henry sniffed the air and thought for a moment.

"Smells like someone left the lid off the glue," he said as he identified the smell, and thought of school art classes where they used the little red and white pots of almond smelling white adhesive, with little plastic spatulas to spread it on the paper.

"Gripfix?" queried Harry, as stepped forward to smell the air.

"Never saw that being used in the factory. Useless stuff! Perhaps they tried it on the bottle labels, and gave up in favour of something else. It would have been before my time though."

He went back and selected another sandwich. Had he been at home he would have been eating his dinner by now, but the sandwiches were a good substitute for the selection of tins in his larder.

The others took their cue from Harry, and attacked the sandwich tray while the dust settled. Eventually Harry picked up the cycle front lamp that he used as a torch, and stuck his head and arm through the hole. Having satisfied himself on the nature of the wall, he picked up the sledgehammer and, taking up a pose much like the start of a J Arthur Rank film, he gave a mighty blow about two courses down from the hole. A large section about a yard wide fell inward into the hole. He retired to the canteen counter while the dust again settled.

Tracey and Reg stepped through the hole, and started to clear the area as best they could. Once it was safe to move about, Tracey approached the nearest shelf, and selected a Fry's Chocolate wholesale box. It was heavy, but with a struggle she heaved it over to the entry for Henry to take from her.

"Couldn't see any glue tubs in there," she gasped, as Henry relieved her of her load. "Might be something in here though."

All four clustered round the table where Henry was opening the box. Inside were booklet-sized packets of paper wrapped in brown paper. As Henry split open a packet Harry gasped. Even before he saw the writing on the front of the muddy red covers.

"Bugger me! Ration books!" he exclaimed.

Henry did a quick count of the booklets in a packet, and a guess at the number of packets in the box.

"God, there's enough here to supply the whole of Peckham. He couldn't use all these without someone noticing."

Unlike Harry, who had spent the war years at sea in the merchant navy, Henry was a small boy when war broke out. But he remembered his mother as she struggled to feed him, and his two sisters, on the meagre rations towards the end of the war. But these were not food ration books, they were for clothing. As if he read Henry's thoughts Harry reached into the box and pulled up the top three layers. There below them were squarer packets, and ripping one open revealed the buff coloured cover of a Ministry of Food ration book.

"Bugger me!" repeated Harry, as he turned the booklet over in his hand.

"Harry," asked Tracey, "What did Strudwick make in the factory during the war? Was he a government supplier?"

"Yes. He still made French polish. And lots of it. I joined in '45, but the blokes who were here during the war told of three shifts, and seven day working during the blitz. He had ministry contracts for a thick grade that they painted on copper coils. It soaked into the cotton covering and made them waterproof. Apparently it was also a favourite finish for coffins, if you'll pardon the pun."

"But I thought at the time there was a shortage of wood?"

"Yes, and French polish on a cardboard coffin gave a bit of dignity to the proceedings. Apparently he made a special grade that gave a reasonable appearance with only one coat."

Tracey shook her head. She had heard of spivs and black market goods from her aunts and uncles, but seeing even this single box and its contents gave her a feel for the scale of things.

Suddenly she burst out laughing. Reg looked puzzled, but Henry seemed to know what she had found funny, and gently joined in. Eventually she stopped, and wiped the back of her hand across her eyes.

"I think I know how to persuade Strudwick to sell us the freeholds," she said, and burst out laughing again.

"At a nominal price?" asked Henry, as he again joined her in her mirth.

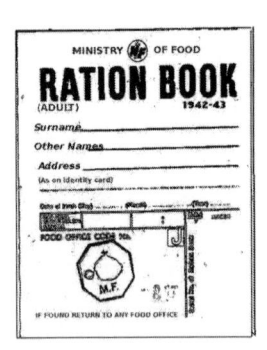

Meanwhile Harry had slipped through the gap into the tunnel and was shining a torch along the shelves. There were a dozen or more boxes, and an ominous-looking tin steamer trunk at the far end of the tunnel. Beyond that was the shelter with eight bunk bed frames and an enamel pail with a lid. Harry tugged at the lid of the trunk but it was either locked or else rusted solid. He walked back towards the canteen, pausing beside two boxes that stood out from the others. They were wooden and had the letters 'WD' and a broad arrow branded on the rough wood. Harry had seen many such boxes when he was in the Merchant Navy, and knew instinctively what they might contain.

"Miss Mulligan!" he called, reverting to a more formal form of address automatically, as he recalled the result when a stevedore had dropped a similar box as they loaded their ship in Liverpool in the summer of 1942.

Tracey looked around for where the voice came from.

"What have you found, Harry?"

"I think it's small arms ammunition!"

"What?"

"Bullets!"

Harry's words got everyone's attention.

"Are you sure, Harry?" called Henry. "There were a lot of empty boxes around after the war. My Mum used one to make a rabbit hutch."

"It's nailed shut and there are no signs that the lid has been disturbed."

"Get out of there, Harry!"

It was Tracey who spoke, and Harry was only too happy to do as he was told.

"Harry, go and get the trolley from the stores. We need to move all paper items to have a good look at later. And Reg, can you give him a hand. There are several empty rooms upstairs where we can put stuff, although it would be nice to be able to lock it away."

"Tom Dawes has an Oxo tin of keys in his room. We should be able to find one to lock a room there."

Henry Fothergill, who had not been party to Reg's nighttime excursions in the factory, frowned as Reg spoke.

"It's okay Henry. Reg has been very helpful to me in the past. Without him we would not be where we are today... Go and see what you can find, Reg."

It was a long night, but by about three o'clock, all the other boxes and cases had been moved to an upstairs room, and a pile of pallets had been stacked in front of the hole in the wall. As the last pallet was heaved into place, Henry suddenly had a horrible thought. How was he going to explain to Jane where he had been? Even worse, what if she asked him whom he had been with!

"Henry, Harry, it's best that you two don't get involved in what we have to do now. Go home, and get some sleep. Take tomorrow, I mean today, off."

Henry nodded and brightened up. His girls would be off to school in a few hours, and for the first time in a long while, he and Jane would have the house to themselves during the day. He might not get as much sleep as a whole day off could otherwise permit.

Tracey smiled and linked arms with Reg. She steered him towards the stairs that lead to her office.

"I think we need to speak to our friends about what we do next. But first we need to tidy up a bit and get some rest."

*****

John Dillon put down his coffee cup and looked up expectantly. DS Holmes smiled as he saw the man sitting beside Tracey at the big brassbound mahogany desk.

"Ah, Terry. Thank you for coming. We have a problem that needs some discrete handling."

Holmes sat down in the vacant chair opposite the pair, and nodded his thanks to Polly as she handed him a cup of coffee. He made a mental note to update his expenses form later.

"How can I help?"

"We've found something, and we are hoping you can relieve us of it without any red tape."

Tracey gave him her best smile as she spoke. Holmes wondered if it was the smile or the caffeine, but something was making him feel a bit hyperactive.

"What is it?"

"We think it's a box of ammunition."

"Oh. What sort!"

"We don't know. We haven't opened it."

"How much?"

"If our stores man is right then probably a thousand rounds or so, depending on the calibre."

Holmes put down his cup, and looked from Tracey to John, straining to see if they were joking.

"Okay, what's the story."

"We were exploring a walled up part of the canteen, and found two wooden boxes. Our storeman, Harry Derry, thinks they are War Department ammunition box, and it looks as if they are still sealed."

"So why call me. Uniform can handle that perfectly well."

"We would prefer it if it was found somewhere else. Somewhere that did not involve the factory. I know it's a big thing to ask, but we have our reasons. Good reasons… Is there anything you can do?"

Holmes thought for a moment then grinned.

"May I use your telephone?"

Tracey smiled and pointed at the Trimphone on her desk.

"And perhaps you could get me another cup?"

John Dillon nodded. It was another way of saying that he needed to make a call in private. He and Tracey got up, and left Holmes to it. When they returned he was making an entry on his expenses form.

"I've got a van coming to pick them up. You'd better show me where the stuff is."

Tracey led him out into the corridor, and down to the canteen. It took a while to remove the stack of pallets and get into the tunnel, but once it was clear, Holmes went in to inspect their find. He noticed the empty shelves with their telltale square dust free shapes and drag marks to their edges.

He came back through the opening, and asked Dillon to get him a brush. Dillon frowned, but went to the canteen counter, and asked the recently arrived Edith for one. She handed it over. Holmes went back inside, and walked the length of the tunnel, dragging the brush along the shelves as he went. After a few passes up and down he was satisfied, and came back out into the canteen.

"Hungry work that," he said as he dusted his arms with his hands. "I've got some friends coming to pick up your boxes. With budgets what they are, they will come in useful at Holborn."

Tracey turned to John for a translation.

"Police firing range," he said simply.

She went to the counter, and returned with a plate of freshly made bacon sandwiches, and more coffee. The three of them sat at a table, waiting for Holmes's men.

Half an hour later Tom Dawes appeared with two men. They looked like police officers, but their uniform was unfamiliar to Tracey. They wore navy blue knitted jumpers and blue berets.

"'D6!" muttered Dillon, and turned to Tracey. "Firearms training unit. Looks like we are bypassing lost property."

One of the two men recognised Dillon, and shook his hand warmly.

"So you've got a present for us. That should make the inspector happy. Let's see what you've got."

The two men slipped through into the tunnel, and stood staring at the boxes. One shook his head, and turned towards the entry.

"Anyone got a crowbar?"

"I'll get one from stores."

Tracey left the four men to fetch one. She returned shortly.

"Damn!" said one of the firearms unit, as he gently prised open the first box. Then, as he opened the second one he continued in a somewhat louder voice. "Everyone leave the building. NOW!"

Dillon was on his feet in an instant, and went straight for the entry to the tunnel, but his path was blocked by the two officers who were coming out very quickly!

"What's up?"

"It ain't rounds. It's bloody plastic, and dynamite: and it's sweating!"

Holmes, upon hearing the officer, had jumped to his feet, and was already ushering the few early factory staff back towards the stairs.

Tracey looked puzzled at why finding plastic in the tunnel should galvanise the officers into such urgent action.

"What's the panic, John? I don't understand. Why does plastic bother them so much? Are they sure it's not condensation? I've never heard of plastic sweating before."

"No, not plastic, plastic explosives, probably Comp B: and that explains the smell. It's the dynamite that's unstable!'

*****

As always on these occasions it started to drizzle, a light, penetrating rain that drifted onto you and got everywhere. Most of the factory staff stood on the pavement well away from the terrace of buildings and the few remaining inside were on their way out to join them.

Tracey and Dillon sat with Holmes in the back of the firearms department van.

"There's a Navy bomb disposal unit on its way from Greenwich, but we need to get our story straight before they get here."

Holmes was in a serious mood, all thoughts of expense claims banished for the moment, despite the opportunities that the situation presented.

"Just why did you call me in the first place?"

"We think we know who put that box there. If he were prosecuted he would turn difficult, and that could jeopardise our plans for the factory. We thought you could help."

Holmes looked quizzically from Tracey to Dillon, clearly seeking a translation.

"Herbert Strudwick! He still owns the freehold, and is threatening to stop us making changes to the building."

"Strudwick! I thought he was dead."

"No. He's been in a coma for two years, and now he's out of it and wants to control the factory."

"And if you upset him, it will cause problems?"

"Yes. We plan a new product range, but it's only viable if we knock down a few walls and make new entries."

Holmes was silent for a while. He instinctively wanted to catch criminals, and possession of explosives could lead to a host of other things. But he was also a practical man. The stuff had been there for years and proving ownership could be difficult. Besides, half the really good arrests he had made since making sergeant were down to information from Tracey.

"Okay. So the stuff was in the abandoned shelter, and you found it by breaking down the door. You only moved it into the tunnel for a better look; and put it down as soon as you had an inkling as to what it might be."

Tracey looked blank, so Dillon explained.

"No proof that Strudwick ever entered the shelter; just used the tunnel for storage."

"Yes, storage!" said Holmes as he looked from one to other of his companions. "I wonder what he stored in those big boxes."

"All we found were papers, and out of date documents."

Tracey gave Holmes one of her best smiles as she spoke, but it had little impact on him. Perhaps he was becoming immune, although having her fiancé sitting beside her probably did not help her deliver the desired effect.

Holmes reached for his pocketbook. Now they had an agreed sequence of events he needed to get something written down before the duty inspector turned up.

The Navy arrived, surveyed the surrounding area, and selected a bombed out site further down the road. Then they conveyed the explosives, one small block at a time, to the centre of the site and used detonators to explode them. By ten o'clock, a crowd of on-lookers had assembled to watch the show, and half a dozen uniform constables were employed to direct traffic and constantly push back the spectators to a safe distance. The last block was removed a few minutes before noon, and Tracey thought they could get back to normal.

"Reg, can you start to track down the staff, and get them back to work?"

"Hold it," said Dillon, "now comes the hard bit."

Tracey looked puzzled, until she saw two naval ratings very carefully carrying one of the boxes in a canvas sling towards the bombsite. The wood of the box would be soaked in explosive, and even the slightest drip onto the pavement would probably explode on impact.

Ten minutes later, the largest explosion of the day rattled windows and threw up a cloud of dust and splinters from the site, as the saturated wood exploded.

Finally the Chief Petty Officer in charge of the squad came back to the van, and gave them the all clear. It was time to try and get the factory back to normal. Tracey sent one polish stirrer along to the Squinting Badger to round up staff, and slowly they drifted back. At about two p.m. Polly found Tracey asleep at her desk. She quietly closed the door, and spent the rest of the afternoon warding off visitors in the outer office.

14. NEGOTIATION

Tracey phoned Catherine Humber, and had a lengthy conversation with her before arranging a second visit to her brother. Catherine, who considered herself worldly wise, was shocked at what they had found. She knew her older brother was a bit of a flyboy, but had no idea he was into serious black market during the war, and certainly could give no explanation as to why he had stolen explosives. She offered to accompany Tracey to see Herbert, so they agreed to meet for lunch in Chiesman's department store in Lewisham, before an afternoon visit.

Tracey had prepared well for the visit and, together with Henry Fothergill, had examined all the packing cases found in the tunnel. To her disappointment the steamer trunk contained mainly a pile of letters addressed to a William Strudwick from various solicitors, and from young ladies whom would have been described at that time as being 'in a predicament'. However, lying in the bottom of the trunk was a Fry's Cocoa tin which held a number of rubber stamps, all copies of various wartime government department imprints.

Although they had only met twice before, the two women got on well. Lunch was pleasant, with Tracey outlining the purpose of her visit as they ate. At first Catherine was defensive of her brother, but as she realised the full impact of what had been found at the factory she fell in with Tracey's plan. While Herbert was making money out of the war, she had been risking life and limb under bombardment in an RAF operations room, and having friend after friend fail to return from action in the skies above Kent. The more she thought about it the madder she got. At one stage she started muttering in a guttural foreign language, unfamiliar to Tracey.

Herbert's private room in Lewisham Hospital, where he was recovering from his hip operation, was clean and bright. They found him sitting in a chair beside his bed, looking out of the window across a grassed area towards the River Quaggy. His appearance had changed a little since Tracey last saw him. Solid food, and some physiotherapy, was beginning to fill him out, and occasional afternoons sitting in the sun had reduced the pallor of his skin.

His attitude towards her, however, had not changed. Even whilst ogling her he began to repeat his warnings about visiting the factory, and about them not making any changes.

"I'm sorry you feel that way, Mr Strudwick," cajoled Tracey sweetly, "as we have come to see you, to see if we can stop you going to prison."

Strudwick relinquished his stare at Tracey's full blouse, and jerked his head up towards her smiling face.

"What?"

"Yes. There has been an incident at the factory, and certain objects came to the attention of the police. We..."

"What objects!" he demanded abruptly.

"Two cases of explosives to start with," replied Tracey.

"You had no right going into the tunnel."

"Well, that's cleared that up," interrupted Tracey with a smile. "At least we now know you knew they were there. Catherine here couldn't believe you were involved."

The old man snorted. It was clear that he was not in control of the meeting. It was a situation he was not familiar with.

"What do you want?" he snapped.

"We'd like to buy the freeholds of the leased parts of the factory, and need answers to a few questions. Oh, but I forgot. I've brought you something to read."

Tracey gave the old man her very best seductive smile as she handed over a copy of H&E magazine. It was a publication that purported to promote health and physical development, allegedly aimed at the naturist fraternity. Tracey's view was that, far from cavorting about unclad in frosty weather, you needed a grubby mac and plimsolls to go with it. It was littered with pictures of nude men and women.

"I think you enjoy this sort of reading. Oh, and this copy comes with two bonus supplements. I know you will be interested in them."

He grabbed the magazine and eagerly opened it. Out fell two booklets. One dirty red and the other buff coloured. He recognised them instantly as coming from the boxes in the tunnel.

"When you have finished with them I can let you have some more. As many as you like!"

The old man's face fell. But then his expression changed to puzzlement.

"What else have you got to say?"

The question took Tracey by surprise. Then she remembered the travel trunk.

"Are we speaking about what we found in the packing cases, or the trunk?"

Herbert's eyes glazed over, but he made no reply. Tracey waited for some time before she continued.

"I have a list here of which parts of the factory are leasehold, and who the freeholder is. I've consulted a valuer, and you will see the figures beside each. However, he also said that the value reflects the limited market interested in them. Given how low his valuations are, I'm therefore prepared to cover both sides of the legal expenses of transfer."

Herbert looked at her, trying to assess his bargaining position. But her smile gave nothing away, and her voluptuous presence only distracted his chain of thought.

"I'm not interested!" he said eventually.

"I thought you might say that, so here is a list showing how the total sum offered will decrease daily over the next three weeks. At the end of that time I will hand over certain items to the police, together with a very full statement about their origin. I believe they have a hospital wing in Wandsworth prison, but I doubt it's as well furnished as this room."

At this point Catherine intervened.

"Be reasonable Herbert. The offer is more than the rent you would get, and you will need money now you are in hospital."

"I understood my medical costs were taken care of."

Tracey grinned before replying.

"Only while you were in St Borgia's. The liability was spelt out very clearly in the sales agreement for the factory. I must compliment Lionel Dee on his thoroughness in drafting the contract sometime."

The old man grunted. He knew when he was beaten; he now needed a face saver before he agreed the deal.

But Tracey stood firm, in body and mind. He put the business to the back of his mind, and enjoyed a long lecherous gaze at her. Standing beside Tracey, his sister scowled.

"All right. But you pay all my legal costs," he said eventually, hoping to find some way to inflate his side of the deal.

But Tracey was well ahead of him.

"Of course. I'll get my solicitors to handle both sides. If you'll just sign this document to confirm that it is an agreed contract, and that as the price is already confirmed, then there is no conflict of interest in their handling it."

She drew a cream foolscap sheet from the voluminous bag that she carried, and handed it to the man. He leant back slightly, forcing her to lean forward towards him as she did so. She understood his intention, and lingered for a moment to ensure her perfume reached him. She did not begrudge him a last peak over the top of her blouse. She was already planning how to leak information to the authorities once the sale was completed, and doubted that his future would include much female company.

As Catherine and Tracey prepared to leave, the old man picked up the magazine. At the door Tracey paused, and turned.

"By the way, where can we contact William Strudwick? He seems to be the freeholder of parts of the factory."

Herbert cackled. "You won't find him. He's gone."

"But someone must have inherited his estate. Surely you can give us some information about him."

Herbert suddenly hoped that he was not completely beaten and perked up.

"You'll not find him. I've no idea where he is."

"No matter. I'll get my solicitor to look for him. He'll probably start by examining your accounts for the '40s and '50s when he was on your payroll. My accountant, Henry Fothergill, was fascinated by the ledgers and account books in the packing cases. I've heard of double entry bookkeeping, but never three sets of accounts. Although Henry said it was common practice in the criminal world. One set for the taxman, one set for prospective buyers of a business, and a true set for themselves."

Herbert, who was beginning to lose the pallor induced by his two-year coma, went white.

"I can speak on his behalf."

"And a letter gifting his freeholds to us would avoid legal costs?"

He knew when he had been out-manoeuvred.

"Yes. I'll do it."

Tracey reached in her bag, and pulled out a pre-typed letter which she presented to him.

"I'll save you the effort. Just sign here, and I'll get you a copy later."

Herbert grunted, and hunted around theatrically for a pen, but Tracey was already unscrewing the cap of her Parker, and giving him one of those knee-weakening smiles.

Once out of the room, Catherine sought the ward sister. She was anxious to learn when her brother would be released from hospital. After the first year that Herbert was in a coma, she and her other brothers had sold his house, and put the money in a trust for him. So despite being wealthy, he had no home, and would probably try to lodge with one or other of his siblings. She was anxious that such lodging should not be with her and her new husband.

On the way through the interminable corridors that eventually led to the public road, Catherine confided her fears to Tracey. Tracey took her arm to show sympathy, and made up her mind to see if she could organise accommodation for him elsewhere. Perhaps Brixton, or even Parkhurst on the Isle of Wight, if Her Majesty deemed it appropriate.

When the two women reached the pavement in Rushey Green they paused, and stood gazing across the road at Swaddlings Baby Shop.

"Herbert's given them a lot of business in his time," said Catherine in a deadpan voice.

It was forced humour to bridge an otherwise difficult moment. Both women could have benefited from a stiff drink, but it was that brief period of the afternoon between lunchtime and evening opening hours.

"John Dillon should be here somewhere," said Tracey. "Can we offer you a lift?"

"Thank you, yes."

They scanned the kerb for Dillon's maroon Morris Oxford. But before they found it, Dillon appeared from behind them.

"I'm just across the road," he said, pointing at a side street. "How did it go?"

Neither woman answered as they crossed the broad road in front of them, but once on the pavement, Catherine turned to him.

"I think Herbert understands his position, and we need say no more on the subject. But I must thank you, even if he doesn't. Had you acted differently, it could have been a very serious outcome for him."

Tracey squeezed John's hand as they approached the car. All in all it had been a successful afternoon, and she was in a mind to celebrate later that evening. A quiet celebration, just for two, and she would phone Polly later to say she was taking tomorrow off.

15. NEW TRICKS, OLD DOGS

Despite working in difficult circumstances, Alfred Potter slowly got an efficient pilot production team together, and was able to demonstrate cost controlled production of a range of 48 colours.

Assembling a full-scale production team was a challenge, even for the indefatigable Potter. A number of staff from other areas were seconded as Tracey prepared for launching the paints on an unsuspecting public. It was not a smooth process, but slowly the newly formed team members came to understand that working for Potter was very different to their old environments. He demanded not just their manual labours, but also mental effort and common sense. These last two had not been exercised very much in their old jobs, and needed considerable practice before they attained anything remotely like a working proficiency. During their training, the initial mistakes made by the Wolves team were repeated in numerous variations, but eventually the full-scale production area was planned in the basement, and builders moved in to make the necessary alterations.

Simultaneously Tracey got Harry Derry to create a set of colour names that were more in keeping with the product, and their intended market. She spent a lot of time consulting him about packaging and marketing. Harry enjoyed the challenge of the work, as well as the frequent contact with Tracey. He was beginning to look on her almost like a lively, fun loving, daughter. He started a list of which of their customers were likely to be interested in the product range.

Harry sat in Tracey's outer office, notes in hand, watching Polly and Susan as they went about their work. There was something about the two that invoked contentment in him. It was almost like watching your own children as they grow and blossom into adults, that you can boast proudly about to friend and stranger alike. When he had an appointment with Tracey he always arrived early, in the hope of a few minutes sat watching the girls.

"Come in Harry, and make yourself comfortable."

As he approached her, his nostrils began to fill with *Evening in Paris*. Frequent meetings had somewhat dulled the flashbacks to his late wife that the scent used to trigger, and he was not surprised when he found himself thinking of Doreen Mulligan instead. He grinned a sheepish grin, but quickly stifled it as he saw Tracey smile knowingly at him.

"First of all I want to thank you for all you have done since I took control of the company. I don't just mean the day-to-day stuff, but all those other things that you've taken in your stride… But tell me, do you think that young Reg is capable of running the stores when you leave? We would get him some help of course, especially with the new range of paints just about to be launched."

Harry's heart sank as he thought of his impending retirement age, and the fact that the factory must function without him after his departure. He had put off thinking about retirement recently. True he was sixty-five in a few months' time, but he had enjoyed work so much of late, and had intended to ask if he could stay on.

"I guess he could do the job. But it might be an idea if I came in, say, once a week to keep an eye on things."

Tracey sat for a moment, as if pondering on what he had said. Then she shook her head.

"I'm afraid that might not be possible Harry… I would think you'll be far too busy."

For the first time ever, Tracey irritated Harry. He had heard others who retired expressing the view that they were as busy as when they were working, but he could not see it in his own lonely circumstances. He resented her presumption, and her smile did nothing to mollify that resentment. If anything it made it worse.

He had hoped that he might have spent some time in Cheshire with Doreen when he retired, and had been up for one weekend with her since she went home. But he had not seen her recently. When he last spoke to her on the telephone, she had seemed preoccupied, and had hinted that she was selling her house, and had plans. She would not give him any details, as she said they was not yet finalised. It looked as if her ardour for him was cooling; a short intense fling which had run its course.

Suddenly all he had to look forward to were a few more weeks with the company, and then an eternity of loneliness. His face went glum, and he struggled to find something to say.

Tracey continued to smile. Then the smile spread to a grin, and she reached forward to lay a hand on his arm.

"I'm sorry Harry, I should have explained. I'd like you to take up the job of marketing the new paint range. If you would stay on, that is. In addition to our existing customers, there are a lot of new opportunities in other areas to explore. I'm afraid it would mean spending some time out with customers, and more time up here with me. There's an office free behind Susan's desk... Please say you will."

Harry was speechless. So much ran round in his head that he did not know where to start. Tracey took his lack of reply as hesitation, and moved her hand gently up and down his arm.

"Please say you will, Harry. If only for six months or so, while we get the paints up and running."

Harry eventually managed to open his mouth. His brain still reeled at the prospect of spending his days with his nose full of her perfume, and a background of the happy girlish chatter of Polly and Susan in his ears.

"Yes!" he said, "I'll stay on."

Tracey exuberantly hugged him, and kissed him on the cheek.

"Right. Go and have a think about what you need to do to ensure Reg can take over the stores, and also start on where, beyond our existing customers, we need to get the product known. I'll tell Henry to organise a desk for your new office. By the way, can you type?"

"No! Well, not very fast anyway."

"I'll get you an assistant. Someone mature, with good office skills, who won't need too much supervision."

Harry nodded, but the mention of getting him a desk occupied his mind. It reminded him that the room she referred to was the one that Herbert Strudwick had set out as a lounge. The one that the staff had always called 'the knocking shop'. He barely heard the rest of what she said, although later when he did recall it, he was a bit disappointed that his assistant was not to be Polly, Susan or someone similar.

Back in the stores, Harry sat and stared out of the window. The store's ginger tomcat, sensing his vacant mood, jumped up and sat on his desk. The animal sat alertly, anticipating an arm to sweep him back onto the floor, but it never came.

Reg came in pushing a trolley laden with tins of paint. He saw his boss gazing out the window, and parked the trolley just inside the door.

"Are you all right, Harry?" he asked anxiously.

"Yes," Harry replied dreamily, "Oh yes."

Reg looked hard, and saw the faint lipstick mark on Harry's cheek. He knew that colour very well, and where the mark had come from.

Reg sniffed the air, as if trying to detect perfume. As he did so he turned his nose upward, and clutched his hands to his chest, imitating the classic Bisto Kids advertisement. Harry, still in a daze, turned to face him. His assistant's comic pose brought him back to earth with a chuckle.

"You've no idea just how all right I am. I'm as all right as I could possibly be."

"So you accepted Tracey's offer then?"

"You knew?"

"Of course. She wanted to be sure you wouldn't turn her down. Mary and I had dinner with her and John Dillon last Monday."

"So when you reminded me that I only had eleven weeks to go, you were trying to find out what I had planned?"

Reg grinned cheekily, and Harry looked round for something to throw at his young assistant. To his surprise, he saw the cat sitting in front of him, and shooed it from the desk. The cat, thinking that things were back to normal, jumped off and ran under the storage shelves. But Harry knew that normality, as he knew it, was gone forever.

"Reg, can you do me a favour?"

"Yes, oh master," Reg replied with a bow, "your wish is my command."

"Daft bugger! No, it's just that I'll have an assistant in my new job. Tracey said that she would find someone mature, with good secretarial skills. But I'd prefer someone more like Polly or Susan. Someone with a bit of life in them, to keep me on my toes. Since you're so pally with her, could you have a word and see if you could persuade her to find me someone younger. I know I'm just a silly old man, but I've sort of got used to the young girlish chatter when I go up to the office. It makes the place seem alive, somehow, and I'd prefer someone like those two helping me. It would help keep me alert."

"She didn't say if she had anyone in particular in mind?"

Harry shook his head, and Reg collapsed into laughter.

"Oh, Harry! Believe me, as far as you are concerned, Christmas is coming early again."

Harry looked at Reg quizzically, but despite his pleas, Reg would say no more on the subject.

16. YULETIDE PREPARATIONS

It was early October, and Tracey called a meeting of senior managers to discuss the annual works outing. It had been a summer institution in the factory, but Ponsonby had cancelled both it and the staff Christmas Party the previous year. Tracey had been unable to do anything about it until she had full control of the factory, but, now with Hardcastle bought out, and in full possession of the freehold to the premises, she decided she would emphasise her management style, and organise a memorable social for the staff. She considered bringing up the subject at the Foremen's meeting, but decided a smaller group would make those present feel more part of a core management team.

Tom Dawes spoke enthusiastically about the last Strudwick's outing when they spent the day in Ostend. But wiser heads pointed out that November and December were not the best times for a long sea crossing. As always Tracey already had something in mind.

"I was thinking of perhaps a weekend event, with a Saturday evening dinner dance and, weather permitting, a few hours walk by the seaside. How about Hayling Island?"

Dawes immediately brightened up at the prospect of a sea voyage and duty free drinking. No one bothered to tell him that Hayling Island was attached to the Hampshire mainland by a bridge.

It was a fairly short meeting. Once Tracey had made a proposal, the others present felt relieved of any obligation to think, and lapsed into their normal bovine state. There was a brief discussion about budgets, but Tracey assured them that as a group they could get an extremely good rate, and the company would subsidise the event by paying half the costs. She smiled inwardly as she remembered a holiday camp manager who owed her a number of favours from when she had privately advised him against the expensive solution that management consultants had recommended, and spent several weekends at the camp helping him to put the business on a sound footing. A date was provisionally set for the first weekend of December; a date that Tracey had already determined was available at the camp.

News of the outing cheered the staff tremendously. The French polish production teams had finally realised that the demand for their product was dwindling, when a local furniture manufacturer cut its monthly order to a fraction of what it had been. There had been talk of short time working and lay-offs. In fact, if two teams had not stopped production to work on setting up the rubber paint line, then Tracey would have been forced to make an unpleasant decision.

As details of the weekend Christmas event filtered down to the staff, the usual excessive, and mainly unnecessary, preparations began to take place. Workers, especially the ladies, began to bring in garments that they intended to wear at the dinner dance, seeking their workmates approval. Several scuffles broke out in the canteen when such approval was withheld, straining long-term friendships for days. Little groups disappeared at lunchtimes as they scoured Rye Lane for items deficient in their wardrobes, and in general everyone was in high spirits.

To the surprise of many, Darren, the young dispatch supervisor, revealed a mastery of ballroom dancing. In desperately looking for a girlfriend, he had joined a dance class. Whilst he had only moderate success in meeting the fairer sex at the classes, he had discovered that he had a natural gift for trotting round a dance floor in musically prescribed fashion. He started to hum as he walked about the loading bay, and perform intricate waltz steps and twirls as he went about his daily work.

Word soon spread about his skill. Initially this was only amongst his team of packers and dispatchers, but soon porters and cleaners would linger about the bay doors in the hope of observing his complicated movements. Staff members began to consult him. He was a man whose time had come.

Darren enjoyed the new attitude of his fellow workers. For years they had looked down on him as a callow, brainless youth. Yet now people sought him out, and asked his opinion of things. This gave him an idea that he hoped would further promote his new status in factory society.

After seeking Tracey's permission, Darren began to give dance classes after work in the canteen. Armed with a Dansette record player, and a stack of long play records, he set up his dance studio at the north end of the canteen. Each afternoon, as soon as the factory stopped work, he would shuffle round the floor chalking out the foot placements for that particular evening's lesson. Assisted by two of his new dispatchers, who cleared the area by stacking tables and chairs to one side, he set up his class for potential pupils.

The class was a success from the start. An odd assortment of male pupils would assemble soon after five o'clock, and spend an hour pacing out over the chalk footprints that he drew on the floor, arms clutching imaginary partners as they went. Like Darren, many of his pupils joined in the hope of attracting a partner of the opposite sex. Given the rather odd nature of some of the staff it could be difficult to determine exactly what was their opposite sex.

Darren's two assistants, Billy and Pat, would man the record player and leap in to renew worn floor marking while Darren appraised and corrected his pupils after each tune.

As the class members became more proficient, some of the bolder pupils began to practice moving their right hand up and down their non-existent partner's backs as they stomped around the room. This was an essential element in the planning of their evening's strategy for the dinner dance, a strategy that required a geographic knowledge of where bra clips and suspender belts were located, if it were to successfully culminate in their social objective.

Two people immune to this activity were Reg Swinton and Harry Derry. Reg was making notes on those activities related to the stores that Harry had previously carried out, and Harry was preparing for his new role. Eventually the agreed date for the move came, and Harry could no longer put off moving upstairs to his office.

As the full impact of the change to his working life became apparent, Harry began to lose confidence in his ability to carry out the new job. So it was with trepidation that he eventually stood up one Monday at about eleven o'clock, shook Reg by the hand, and then gathered together his few personal possessions in a cardboard box. He had wondered if he could put off the move until after lunch, but felt that he really did need to put in an appearance that morning.

As he wended his way through the maze that made up the factory Harry's thoughts were decidedly glum. Over the weekend he had made several attempts to phone Doreen from the call box at the end of his street, but to no avail. On the last attempt an automated voice had told him that the number was disconnected.

He had grown fond of his young assistant, Reg, and today he was moving to a new job, in new surroundings, separated from his work of three decades and his familiar surroundings. He wondered if he was doing the right thing as he looked forward to his sixty-fifth birthday.

It was a very despondent Harry who finally climbed the stairs to the management suite, alone and unsure of his ability to do the job. He was beginning to have severe doubts about his capacity to learn new skills, and he wondered if he would not have been better off retiring, seeking that little bungalow at Dungeness that he had always dreamt of.

As he reached the landing, the scent of *Evening in Paris* seeped into his nostrils, and he cheered up a little. The weak scent grew stronger as he opened the outer office door.

Polly looked up from her typing, her happy face breaking into a smile as she saw him approach.

"Hello Harry, we expected you earlier. Your assistant has been in since nine o'clock."

In other circumstances that smile and cheery greeting would have gladdened Harry's heart, but today he felt he was in uncharted waters, vulnerable to whatever fate threw at him.

In the corner of the room, Susan giggled. Harry presumed that it was at the reference to some efficient, but severe matron that Tracey had found to assist him, and who would be impatiently awaiting her tardy boss with a vexed expression. Personally he could see nothing to amuse him as the full reality of meeting his assistant and starting work hit him. Reluctantly he walked past Susan and opened the inner door to his new office. As he did so the smell of perfume grew stronger still.

Harry was speechless. There, sitting at a second desk in the room, her hair tied up in a bun with a pencil thrust through it, was his new assistant. The desk faced towards his own new desk, and away from the door, but even from behind Harry suddenly knew what Reg meant by the phrase 'Christmas coming early'.

"It's about time you showed up Harry Derry, I was getting bored here, left on my own with nothing to do," she said, as she stood and turned to face him.

Harry carefully closed the door to the outer office behind him, and advanced towards Doreen.

17. SEASONAL CELEBRATION

On the Monday of the week before the Christmas dinner dance, Henry Fothergill posted up an accommodation chart, from the holiday camp, in the canteen. Staff crowded round it eagerly, in order to lay claim to their preferred chalets. There was a mix of two bed, four bed and six bed units. Faced with the chart, many realised that there was a certain amount of planning to perform before placing pen to paper. Once a claim had been staked, then it was open to public scrutiny, and some were not willing to declare their intentions to the world at large. Therefore a certain amount of negotiation and subterfuge began to take place.

Couples wishing to privately share a chalet, but without other workers, or more particularly family members, learning of their intention, realised the danger of a public declaration; they found themselves seeking out other like-minded pairs with the purpose of claiming two chalets for fictitious single sex occupancy. Negotiations went on for several days, with much intense communication, and in some cases inducements offered, before most were satisfied with their publicly displayed accommodations. Even on the Thursday evening there were still a handful of unhappy people shown lodged in the six berth single sex chalets, and with little prospect of turning the booking into fiction.

As well as accommodation there was the question of travel. A few older staff, relying on memory of previous visits to the area, planned to travel by train to South Hayling, and walk the short distance to the camp.

On the Friday afternoon, as some ninety people queued for a cheap weekend return at Peckham Rye, the ticket office clerk patiently informed them that there was no such station, it having closed in 1963. The ensuing heated debates resulted in long delays, and a number of staff missing their intended trains.

Eventually all rail passengers were on their way to Havant, to continue their journey from there by bus or shared taxi. A small number of more enterprising staff, who had their own transport, offered to share travel expenses with less fortunate colleagues. All such spare places were eagerly solicited, again with appropriate inducements.

One polish stirrer, who possessed a driving licence, had an uncle who owned a van that was not used during the weekends. Upon announcing its availability, he quickly found eight passengers for his journey. They travelled sitting in deckchairs and on crates for a circuitous journey, arriving long after the dining room had closed for the Friday evening. He had neglected to tell his passengers that his uncle was a fishmonger. After several hours in the enclosed metal rear of the vehicle, most felt sympathy for sardines in cans, as by then they were sure they had shared a similar experience.

By nine o'clock most of the attendees had settled in. A queue formed at the telephone boxes as youngsters, away from home on their own for the first time, rang parents to assure them that they had arrived safely: and to emphatically deny that they had any knowledge of specific other youngsters whom their parents suspected to be away from home that same weekend. Often, said other youngster would be huddled against the wind in the phone box as the call took place, stifling giggles as they followed the conversation with their bodies entwined, and heads either side of the telephone handset, awaiting their turn to make a similar call home.

A few longer established couples, living at home with parents and starved of privacy for most of the year, dispensed with such preliminaries, and retired immediately to darkened chalets to enjoy each other's company in private.

Many others assembled in the bar or ballroom. The party which arrived by van were easily identifiable by their newly washed, wet, hair and heavy application of Brut, Old Spice or Hai Karate - with just a faint undertone of kippers.

Darren's pupils, eager to display their newly learnt skills, cajoled partners to join them in the ballroom. There they found that the process was considerably harder than during their practice sessions, with a second pair of feet attempting the same perambulation in close proximity. Many retired to the side tables, either hurt or in a vain attempt to ply liberal doses of medicinal alcohol to injured partners. A rare few did impress their partners sufficiently to progress on to their right-handed geographic exploration, for which two were subsequently rewarded by experiences that they would remember for a considerable time, and one received a black eye which he was going to find hard to explain to his parents.

Two groups of French polish stirrers from the Millwall and Crystal Palace teams quickly decorated their chalet windows with the emblems of their chosen teams. Then they set forth upon their quest to put in the requisite number of hours of steadfast drinking that true team support dictated.

Alfred Potter and Edith from the canteen had no qualms about declaring their relationship. They retired to their thin walled chalet and enjoyed each other's company so energetically that the green-coated entertainment staff were dispatched several times to warn them about making excessive noise. Eventually, about eleven o'clock that evening, the exhausted pair sought the bar for a nightcap, and a rest before resuming activities.

On Saturday morning, many members of the group missed breakfast, and few surfaced much before mid-morning. Exceptions to this were Tracey Mulligan, John Dillon, Reg Swinton and Mary Fluke, who were up early enough for a short walk along the seafront before breakfast. Reg and Mary were early enough for a longer walk, but the weather beat them back after a brief glimpse of the white crested waves with the wind whipping foam from their tops to float on the wind like bubble bath.

Back in the dining hall, Harry Derry and Doreen Mulligan joined the four as they finished their cornflakes and porridge. For the sake of modesty Reg, Harry, Mary and Doreen had entered into a fictitious accommodation plan, but Tracey and John had a publicly declared superior suite not much smaller than her flat in Peckham.

Over a leisurely meal, the six of them chatted about life in general, including Tracey and John's wedding plans. Reg and Mary sat quietly holding hands under the table, and sneaking glances at each other as the conversation rolled round. Eventually Mary could contain herself no longer.

"Reg and I are getting engaged on Christmas Eve."

The conversation stopped. All eyes turned to the couple and after a moment's thought, congratulations were offered. There was only one small dark spot in their happiness.

"Have you told your mother?" asked Harry.

Reg shook his head. He had thought about that very thing for some time. His mother was still living in Spain and unbelievably still did not seem to know the true nature of Ernshaw's drugs, smuggling and prostitution empire out there.

Dillon looked across the table at Mary. He had moved from uniform general duties to run the district training school before she came to Peckham as Maria Gomez, and he was not in a position to compare her appearance then to how she looked now, but he was uneasy about her getting away with fooling Reg's mother for long.

After all, for several weeks she was the maid in a house where Mrs Swinton was a guest. She was being very careful to maintain her shorthaired blonde appearance, and every so often she smelt of bleach as she re-treated her eyebrows, but it was a masquerade that he was not sure she would be able to carry on forever.

He made a mental note to catch up on Ernshaw's current location and residual activities in the UK. The last he had heard was that the man was still in a Moroccan prison, and that the regional crime squad had raided the Silwood Street arches. But the man still had contacts that would be eager to please him with the small task of eliminating one, or even two, victims.

Breakfast over, the couples went their separate ways. Despite the more physical examples all around them, Reg and Mary were building their relationship more slowly, with the emphasis on snuggling up together and light petting. They also spent much time talking about the future. Had Dillon been asked to express an opinion he might have suggested that they had only a very short future if they remained in Peckham.

Throughout the day, groups and couples enjoyed the facilities of the camp, and the surrounding island. Balls clicked on snooker tables, lighter ones pinged on the table-tennis courts and much splashing was heard from the indoor swimming pool. By five o'clock though, the camp quietened down as rest and recuperation prepared the merrymakers for the evening to come.

The dinner-dance was a great success. It lacked the character of the previous such event two years ago when Lionel Dee had booked a newly opened Greek Taverna in Forest Hill, but it was well executed by experienced staff. Like the previous event, the menu was based on poultry meat, in this case from the vast battery farm on the island. Unlike the previous event, it was a traditionally cooked meal recognisable by all. The accompanying drink was palatable, and lacked the dire aftereffects of the industrial spirit and fruit juice concoctions of the earlier event.

However, some of the more ardent football supporting polish workers considered it a duty to consume their dinner primarily in liquid form, and Tom Dawes had an ad hoc team patrolling all evening, removing drunks from the ballroom, as and when necessary. Consequently his own meal was eaten in short snatches while supervising their activities, and the ensuing indigestion remained with him for the whole of the next day.

Before the meal, Tracey welcomed all and made a few announcements. The company name was to change to *Peckham Paints*, as of February in the coming year, and in addition to paints the company would start producing a number of other products.

She also formally announced several staff changes, including Reg Swinton as storeman with two assistants, Harry Derry as product marketing manager, Henry Fothergill as a director, and Tom Dawes as a director. Tom's promotion came as a complete surprise to him, and he professed himself undeserving of the honour. Privately Tracey agreed, but she wanted to install the much more dynamic Alfred Potter as general production manager.

The band were a bit bland, but competent and versatile, and those who had survived, or avoided, Darren's pupils' efforts, were mostly still on the dance floor as midnight approached. Darren found himself consulted continuously by one student or other. Whilst he would have liked to join the quest for dance partners, he enjoyed the attention and the drinks that regularly appeared at his elbow, so he sat and pontificated all evening. Besides, he had low expectations for himself, and preferred not to risk being publicly rejected in front of his pupils.

Men outnumbered women by three to one in the factory, and singles hoping to find romance away from the work environment were in a similar ratio. Darren's pupils had approached almost every single woman as midnight drew nigh, with mixed results. One young dispatch worker, Jenny, was approached by all the would-be dancers, and politely refused each one. She spent the evening gazing at the carpets and chandeliers in the ballroom, making a single glass of Bacardi and Coke last the whole night.

As men and women dragged their preferred partners on for the last slow smooch of the night, Mary whispered in Reg's ear. He hurriedly checked in his pocket for a fifty pence piece and scurried off to the gents in search of a condom machine. Mary sat and waited for his return before taking his hand, and steering him out into the dark towards their chalet. She had decided that it was time for their slow steady romance to enter a new phase.

Sunday morning began much the same as Saturday. Few made it to an early breakfast, and some missed it altogether. Tracey, John, Harry and Doreen sat expectantly waiting for Reg and Mary, but the young couple were otherwise engaged until mid-morning. Instead Henry and Jane Fothergill joined them and for once, Henry was a major contributor to the conversation. Even Jane, who deliberately sat herself between Tracey and Henry, joined in heartily. She had clearly decided that Tracey was not the threat she had earlier supposed. Little did she know how close Tracey had once come to proving her original opinion of her to be correct.

The table took their time over their meal. As they sat there, they watched a few couples openly declaring previously clandestine affiliations to the public. There were a few surprises for the alert diners, especially as some apparently hardened football fans appeared without their usual team badges, and exhibiting very courteous behaviour to unexpected female companions. Tracey made a note of their names. Perhaps they were ready to leave French polish behind to become part of her second paint production team.

Just before the last of the toast was consumed, John Dillon got up and made a phone call. He came back smiling. He had just spoken to DS Holmes. He wanted to find out the current position regarding Ernshaw's gang, and had called Holmes late the night before to make enquiries. This morning Holmes assured him that most of the gangsters were now paying their debts to society, thanks to Fingers Fisher's and Bald Peter's ever-increasing memory recall. There was a warrant out for Ernshaw, should he ever try to return to the UK.

Almost as an afterthought, Holmes had asked Dillon if he had ever met Herbert Strudwick.

"No, never. Why?"

"Oh, just one of those little coincidences in life. You and Tracey went to some lengths to prevent him being prosecuted over those explosives, and now he's been and got himself arrested for fraud by Inland Revenue. Something about avoiding supertax by inventing imaginary employees."

Dillon grinned, and was glad that the telephone did not transmit images. He remembered Tracey phoning a tax inspector the day after the purchase of the freeholds was completed. What he did not know was that Catherine Humber, furious at her brother's wartime behaviour, and determined that she and her new husband would not play host to the lecherous old man, had beaten Tracey to it by an hour.

The weather quickly improved, as it can in coastal areas when the wind drops, but the sea was still very rough, so few ventured out for too long. Lunch was a hot and cold buffet accompanied by a small swing band and a joke-telling compere. Diners seemed to be divided into two groups: couples whom had spent much time out of the public eye tucked in avidly to restore their depleted energy levels, whilst heavy drinkers who had binged since Friday night avoided the greasy chips, fatty pork pies, lamb chops and Irish stew in favour of dry rolls and strong black coffee.

Over lunch, much discussion took place as travellers negotiated transport to Havant railway station, and pairs of couples concocted elaborate stories of how they had spent their time, in case their parents got together to compare notes later. A few of the couples, those who had left it late to make their arrangement, realised at this point that whatever stories they invented would be hard to believe back home. One example of a polish stirrer from the Millwall team allegedly sharing with a Crystal Palace supporter twice his age sounded particularly dubious.

By two o'clock the camp was deserted, and the platform of Havant station was thronged with an unexpected number of would-be passengers. All agreed that it had been a wonderful time, all except the heavy drinkers that is. Many of them had difficulty remembering what sort of time they had had. As a chill wind blew along the platform, they slowly came out of their alcoholic haze to stand wondering how the hell they came to be in Hampshire, instead of at home watching the Sunday afternoon football on television.

The pile of luggage stacked where the guards' van was supposed to stop had to be rapidly dragged the length of the platform when the train arrived, and revealed that Sunday service was a half-length set of four carriages. Upon boarding, the party found that the train, which started its journey at Portsmouth, had most seats already taken. Many grumbled as they stood squashed together in the corridor, squabbling over each vacant seat as other passengers got up to depart. The young couples, however, had no complaints. Packed together in the corridors, they had a legitimate excuse for a further hour of further bodily contact, with arms around each other ostensibly to provide mutual support as the train rocked and bumped along the track. A few of Darren's students, under the cover of unbuttoned overcoats, took the opportunity for further practise in right-handed geography.

18. CHRISTMAS COMES EARLY

Monday mid-morning saw the canteen full of happy people. There was a buzz as the canteen assistants, and two redheaded staff from the loading bay, put up paper chains and adorned tables with little red tablecloths and artificial tree decorations. Stacks of mince pies had appeared on platters and, after confirming that Mary rather than Edith had made them, they were rapidly consumed. In addition to the mince pies, Tracey had instructed Edith and Mary to clear as much stock as possible preparatory to moving the canteen upstairs early in the new year.

Stocks of tinned corned beef of indeterminate age were turned into a passable hash. Cheese and potato pie arrived on the menu to clear a Cheddar mountain that Ponsonby acquired when he had bought a bankrupt dairy farm's stock at a knock down price, and stocks of condensed milk went into interminable rice puddings.

Edith had misgivings about the changes, but became more receptive after learning that they were to allow the creation of a paint production line, run by Alfred Potter. It was assumed that she and Alfred had talked over the subject of an evening, although if the weekend dinner dance experience was anything to go by, it was hard to imagine the couple refraining from more energetic pursuits long enough for any really meaningful conversation to take place.

Mary, having announced her intended engagement to Reg, did spend some time in deep and meaningful thought. Reg, having shared a new and wonderful experience with her on the Saturday night, wondered why her ardour had cooled somewhat, but was reassured later in the week. Mary resolved to build a new image of herself that was so strong as to cause any previous contact to dismiss any physical resemblance to the maid, Maria Gomez, as mere coincidence.

To this end, Mary spent much of her time phoning Milly in Devon. She planned to acquire a strong Devon accent, and a vocabulary to match. Milly understood her intention, and entered into the spirit of the enterprise. She bought a cassette tape recorder, and searched the library in Torquay for older local authors who used much dialect in their books. Patiently she read these aloud, exaggerating the pronunciation where she could, and compiling a glossary as she went.

Mary listened to the tapes Milly sent, and practised the accent and unfamiliar words each evening. She also took to reading Thomas Hardy's works, particularly *Tess of the d'Urbervilles* where he used much regional dialogue.

To complete the illusion, she invented a brother in Plymouth and two turkey-farming cousins in Moretonhampstead. Milly, knowing that Mary was working in the factory canteen, sought recipes from her local Women's Institute on the pretext of wanting to provide as many authentic local dishes as possible for her guests.

Reg looked puzzled when Mary received a Christmas card from one of her fictitious cousins: a charity card sold in aid of the Donkey Sanctuary at Seaton. It came complete with a short note on the back about how busy they were on the farm with Christmas approaching. When she saw the postmark was Milly's home hamlet of Longcombe Cross, Mary collapsed in a fit of giggles. Next day she took it to work, and stood it on the shelf behind the serving counter, for all to see.

Mary was delighted when a bundle of twenty recipes arrived. She started by trying them out on Reg before persuading Edith that they should put pasties, clotted cream, white pudding with swede and leg of mutton marinated in scrumpy on the menu. Edith was the first to notice Mary's subtle change in accent and odd words. Mary explained that when she arrived in London she was anxious to fit in, and be understood. She claimed that she had found that many of the factory workers, part deafened by constant machinery noise, could understand her better when she imitated the local accent.

By Christmas Eve, Mary was addressing customers as *my dearie* and *me 'ansom*, much to the amusement and pleasure of all she spoke to. She apologised when customers queried *coles* written up on the menu board instead of cabbage, saying it was her *granfer's* fault as she spent most of her childhood summers at their cottage on the moors.

At first, Reg was concerned by her efforts to cast herself as a Devon girl. He remembered how when he first met her she was posing as a Spanish maid, with a reputation as a serious knife fighter. But the more he thought about it, the more he realised that it was a necessary measure to ensure their continued happiness. Besides, he developed a liking for liver casserole, Devon bread with caraway seeds and revel cake. He also noticed that since Mary had moved in with him he had put on half a stone, despite all the running around and lifting at work.

*****

Reg was not the only person to be putting on weight. Harry Derry was finding that Doreen's skills extended beyond the office and bedroom. Her bacon pudding with sage, and her pork pies with nutmeg, were a far cry from the tinned Irish stew, or beans with sausages straight from the tin, that had been the mainstay of his evening meals. She had nominally lodged at Tracey's flat, but spent her weekends, and at least two weekday nights every week, with Harry in his little two-bed terrace.

Doreen's regular and continued presence in Nunhead had an added benefit for Harry. For several years he had been pursued by a vinegary spinster neighbour who had decided he should not live alone, and that she should be his companion. Seeing Doreen's lace trimmed lingerie hanging on the washing line together with Harry's St Michael Y-fronts turned this woman from a constant pest into an instant prude who shunned him, although doubtless she would have been happy had it been her own, less fashionable, smalls sharing the line with his for all the world to see.

At work, Harry soon settled to organising labelling and containers for their new paint products, while Doreen created press releases and articles for the trade papers and other outlets that Harry felt appropriate. As he fell into a comfortable routine with Doreen he began to feel that he had overlooked something. What had started as a casual short time fling had evolved into a long-term relationship, an essential part of his life. He was happy with the relationship: very happy indeed, but something was missing.

One bright sunny Saturday, as he cupped his second mug of breakfast tea in his hands to warm them, and scanned the morning paper for items of interest, he noticed the date. He lifted his head and gazed across the table at the woman who was bringing so much enjoyment back into his life. He realised what it was that made his happiness less than complete.

"This is going to sound silly, but there is someone I think I need to introduce you to."

Doreen looked up from her toast.

"Sure. Who?"

"My Lizzy."

Doreen sat silently studying his face. It had changed from the contented half smile that he had worn since she woke him, to an anxious expression. It was as if he was worried that she would object to the introduction. He had told her his wife was dead, so she waited patiently for him to elaborate.

"I'm probably daft, but I'd like to think that you two would have been friends."

"You mean happy to share you over your lifetime, rather than me take you away from your memories of her?"

Harry nodded. Tears welled up in his eyes, and he would have had difficulty speaking at that point. Doreen decided he needed time to compose himself.

"Let me go and get changed. We'll leave the washing for now."

Harry finished his tea, and waited while Doreen stayed upstairs for as long as she judged he needed. When she came down she had changed from slacks and thick jumper, into a smart dress and jacket.

"How far are we going?" she asked.

"Not far. About ten minutes' walk."

Harry and Doreen paused before the stone pillars and cast iron railings that guarded the entrance to Nunhead Cemetery. It was a grand Victorian complex, filled with elaborate memorials and monuments in the older part. Doreen sensed his apprehension and slipped her arm through his. She held him tightly, giving the impression to the casual observer of clinging to him for support, rather than actually providing it.

They walked along the broad central avenue, between two rows of towering lime trees, towards the imposing chapel, where they turned left onto a narrow asphalt footpath. It was a long path, but eventually Harry turned again onto a short gravel strip. Doreen had not seen such an ostentatious cemetery before, but the Victorian grandeur lapsed into modest rows of graves as they walked further from the central road.

Harry stopped and turned to face a simple plot: a white stone slab and shallow kerb around an oblong of green stone chippings. He bent and pulled a solitary chickweed from the chippings. Its single presence suggested that it was not long since someone last tended the grave, and Doreen instinctively knew that person had been Harry.

She stood behind him, and gently laid a hand on his shoulder.

"How long were you married?"

"Twenty-nine years, and courting for five years before that. But we grew up in the same street, and went to school together."

She stood and read the inscription.

Maude Elisabeth Derry
8th July 1904 - 13th December 1958
'My wonderful wife, taken before her time'

Doreen slipped her hand under his armpit as he rose, then held his hand with both of hers while he stood beside her.

"She never liked the name Maude. I originally called her Elisabeth, but she was always on the go. One day I called her Busy Lizzy, and the name stuck. It was on our honeymoon in Dymchurch."

"Oh, Harry. You should have told me it was today. I'd have got some flowers."

Then she turned back towards the grave, and bent to smooth a few chippings. As she did so she whispered to the headstone.

"I'll look after him for you, Maude Elizabeth. Just the way you would have wished to yourself."

They stood for a while, the sun reflecting on the chippings, and the world at peace around them.

"You were right to bring me here. I do hope she would have approved of me... Tell me all about her on our way home."

With that, Harry turned and led her back towards Linden Grove. On the way he spoke of his Lizzy at length, for the first time since her death, and Doreen listened silently as they walked arm in arm.

Back at Harry's house there was little left to say, but Doreen encouraged him to get out his photo album, and they spent the afternoon leafing through it. It was a strange experience for her, like talking about a distant, vaguely remembered, but fondly loved, relative. For Harry it was more of a coming to terms with life as it really was. The house held so many memories, and he had not changed a thing since her passing. Now he felt ready to move on, and planned to start with a bit of decorating over the Christmas period.

That evening they sorted out a number of Lizzy's possessions that Harry had not previously felt able to part with. Suddenly they no longer seemed important, and Harry could see that their continuing presence might make Doreen uneasy.

As he fell asleep that night, he slipped into a dream where he was walking with Doreen and Lizzy on either arm. The two women were chatting happily to each other, and as the dream faded their faces faded as well, so he could no longer decide which was on which side of him. But he knew that each, in her own way, planned to take care of him.

19. GOODWILL TO ALL MEN

It was a few days before Christmas, and the staff were all in a festive mood. Edith, getting happier and more chatty as each day went by, most definitely entered into the Christmas spirit. One morning she came in early, long before the canteen started to serve customers. By the time Mary arrived, she had pinned bunches of mistletoe every yard or so along the ceiling above where the queue formed at the counter, with an especially large bunch directly above where she stood to serve.

Word spread rapidly, and soon groups of men were heading for the canteen. A technique quickly developed, where twos and threes stood around talking before taking their position in the queue with a precision that ensured an unsuspecting pretty girl in front, behind, or, for the truly expert, both fore and aft as they approached the hanging bunches that provided the excuse for abandoning normal inhibitions.

Reg Swinton first saw the queue placement technique being practised by the Millwall supporting polish manufacturing team in their workshop. Those playing the role of ladies wore dusters as headscarves. Unaware of the purpose of the exercise, the experience shook Reg deeply, and he quietly retired to the stores for a sit down. It was only when Harry came back from a mug of tea, with lipstick on both cheeks and his nose, that the true purpose of the exercise was revealed to him.

At first he was relieved to make sense of what he had seen, but relief quickly turned to panic at the thought of hordes of polish stirrers descending upon Mary's workplace, with the sole intention of embracing whoever they could find in a skirt. He jumped up, and raced to the canteen.

The scene he saw there was little short of carnage. Mary had retired behind the counter, to the safety of the food preparation area. Edith had taken up a position at the counter, with a necklace of paper chains, and an Alice band decorated with sprigs of holly and a Father Christmas on a sleigh. Faced with this sight, some of the younger workers had foregone their morning break, whilst a few of the older men were on their second or third mug.

Alfred Potter had arrived while a particularly amorous foreman was taking very full advantage of Edith's offer. Potter barged his way along the extended queue, and grabbed the man by the back of his collar. With a roar he jerked him backwards, and a scuffle began.

As the foreman began to get the worst of it, his team leapt to his defence. Edith, seeing that the odds had shifted to four to one against Potter, rushed to his side with her two wooden spoons held high. Like a traditional barroom scene from an old cowboy film, various others joined in on one side or other, welcoming an excuse to settle old scores.

Eventually Tom Dawes arrived, grabbing individuals from the edge of the fight and ordering them back to work under fear of dismissal. Bit by bit he dwindled down the combatants until there were just the original four against Potter and Edith. Despite being outnumbered, Potter's prowess with his fists, and Edith's skill using the spoons as clubs, meant that the pair were ahead on points, and it took Dawes only a moment to end the fracas.

When Tracey got to hear of the fracas she summoned those involved to appear in her office in groups of five.

As each group traipsed sheepishly in they saw a large sack on the floor. After a lecture about behaviour at work, Tracey told the group that it was a sacking matter. Each one was then told to return to her office in thirty minutes, with a gift-wrapped toy for the children of families supported by the Salvation Army. Tracey made it clear that failure to do so was not an option if they wished to remain in her employ. Either she got a full sack of toys or else... The choice of container for the toys said all that needed to be said, and there was no need to labour the point.

As a major instigator of the trouble, Potter was ordered to supply two toys, and Edith was lectured on curbing her amorous ways. As Tracey spoke to her, Edith burst into tears. Tracey adopted a more conciliatory tone, and spent some time calming her down. As she probed, Edith confided that since meeting Potter she had become menopausal, and had sought hormone replacement therapy. Apparently the medicinal effect had been heightened by several nights of partying with Potter's friends in the past week, and in consequence she had difficulty controlling her moods and desires. She assured Tracey that she would be back to normal once Christmas was over, and her alcohol consumption reduced to its usual level.

At the end of the day, Tracey's sack was full. She phoned John Dillon to ask him to help transport her offering. That evening they drove to Denmark Hill, where the Sally Ann major in charge at William Booth College was overwhelmed by the spontaneous generosity of her workforce.

In order to go some way towards restoring goodwill to all men Tracey announced that the factory would finish work at noon on Christmas Eve, and a cold buffet lunch would be available.

It was mainly the foremen who took up the offer, some of whom hoped for a repeat of Edith's affections, but after two alcohol-free days she was somewhat subdued.

20. A NEW BEGINNING

One of the first changes Tracey had introduced when she took total control of the factory had been to improve conditions of employment. She arranged for a local GP to offer all staff an annual medical, and increased annual holiday from a flat two weeks by an additional day per four years' service.

The increased holiday was warmly welcomed, but the offer of medical attention treated with scepticism. Surely it was the boss trying to find out who had what, and that worried several who only kept their jobs because others covered for them in one way or another. Tom Dawes broached the subject with Tracey, who assured him that the doctor in question would have sole access to the medical records, except for disclosure to the worker's own GP if there was a need for referral. This went some way to allaying their fears, but it was only after the first round of medicals had taken place, and a few had been sent for further treatment for previously undiagnosed conditions, that the benefit was fully accepted.

Many of the workers, especially those with young families, chose to take their extra days between Christmas and New Year. Some older staff thought them mad, since the factory was very quiet during that period, and any escape from in-laws and a diet of dead turkey was a welcome relief. In general little happened until the first week in January, but that was not to say that things were not being planned.

A set of empty upstairs offices were knocked together to form the new canteen, and Tracey went shopping with Mary and Edith for suitable equipment to install in it.

On New Year's Eve, Tracey invited her friends to dinner. She preferred formal dinner parties to the increasingly popular casual affairs, where prawn vol-au-vents tended to get trodden into the carpets, and red wine spilt on cream soft furnishings.

Catherine and Sam Humber were included amongst those friends, and Sam's roaring laugh was heard loudly, and frequently, throughout the evening. Mary was proudly showing off her shiny new engagement ring, and Doreen let slip that she had given up the pretence of staying with Tracey. It was a poorly held pretence after she had borrowed the firm's van to move her belongings in any case. Neither she nor Harry could drive, and they had persuaded young Darren to perform that task. The loading bay staff had taken great delight in spreading the details throughout the canteen.

All who gathered to celebrate the New Year noticed the estate agent's board propped in the lounge window. Tracey was about to move in with John Dillon. The move was deeply significant. For Tracey it marked a complete break with her past, especially her numerous contacts and customers from her days at Executive Services. Those who had occasion to walk past the Town Hall, and look up, would have also noticed that the office above the adjacent shops was empty, and the 'Executive Services' sign removed. The New Year was definitely a new beginning for many in the room.

On Monday, 5th January, Mary and Edith arrived early at work for their first day in the new canteen. Several rooms had been opened up to form a large eatery, interrupted by a series of supporting columns. It was light, bright and had a headroom several feet taller than the basement they had become used to. The kitchen was smaller than before, but was well equipped with modern appliances, and a small electric hoist to a storeroom directly below it.

Some of the workforce were less impressed than the canteen staff. There were no dark corners to skulk in, and some kept forgetting where the new facility was. It was not until Henry Fothergill pinned signpost-like notices at strategic points throughout the building that some sort of normality was restored. Some of the older staff continued to grumble, on the basis that it was unnatural to go upstairs to eat. One went so far as to suggest that the increased altitude affected his digestion, and thought he should get some sort of compensation. He neglected to remind anyone that he lived on the eleventh floor of a tower block.

To emphasise their new product range, Tracey had instructed the decorators to use the factory's own rubber paints on the walls and ceiling. The effect was most striking, almost Scandinavian, with vivid blue and red doors vying for the diners' attention with walls in more subtle shades of green and cream. Even the chairs had been refurbished in yellows and purples, with pink and blue vinyl seat covers.

Meanwhile in the basement, Potter, and his enlarged team, were installing their production equipment. Numerous arguments broke out around the subject of what football team the paint producers should support. The initial two who supported Wolverhampton Wanderers pressed a claim based on early membership of the new crew, but not everybody was happy to abandon existing allegiances for the black and gold.

Potter was made of sterner stuff than their previous leaders, and to subdue argument suggested that they abandon their past for a higher plane. He organised mechanic's style boiler suits with a Union Jack emblem on the back, and individual names on the left breast. He insisted that in future only the national English team was worthy of their consideration. He engendered an attitude of elitism over the older polish producing teams. This fired the imagination of the workers, and so the issue was resolved. It was only much later when they realised that there were far fewer national side matches per year to debate that some realised that Potter also had productivity in mind.

Potter proved to be a much more alert leader than they were used to. The few intelligent team members were encouraged to perform the more precise operations, whilst others found themselves permanently on menial tasks. As the equipment was installed, and brought into production, he ran the works much like the boiler room of an ocean-going liner. There were a few resignations by long term staff who had difficulty coming to terms with the concept of working a whole day, without numerous extended smoking breaks, and absences while doing a bit of shopping.

Upstairs, in his new office, Harry Derry spent his days telephoning decorating suppliers and other trade customers to push the new range, whilst Doreen typed letters on new stationery to the trade press. The long Christmas break had given Harry and Doreen time to get over the novelty of living and working together, and Harry was beginning to limit himself for the sake of his sciatica. Together they worked well, and orders for the new products began to trickle in.

Reg also settled in his role in charge of the stores, and cautiously accepted the two assistants that Tracey had found him. One was from the Crystal Palace supporting polish team, and the other a school leaver who turned out to be Darren's younger brother, Brian. Neither were over-blessed mentally, and Reg's role rapidly shifted from active work to full-time supervision.

On the loading bay, Darren was also struggling to control his team. Billy O'Keefe was a good worker as long as you gave him tasks that taxed his muscles rather than his brain, and his twin brother, Pat, was almost as physical, but with a degree of intelligence as a bonus. Together they worked well, Pat writing dispatch labels from order forms, and Billy running around packing boxes and loading the van.

Despite his obvious intelligence, Darren found communication with Pat difficult. He had a tendency to respond to questions with a quote from Shakespeare or Byron, leaving Darren to interpret a stanza into the one word 'yes' or 'no' that the question deserved.

Darren very quickly realised the seriousness of his mistake in employing Jenny Wellbeloved, when she brought in a giant wind-chime to hang from the ceiling of the loading dock. That same day, she advised Darren that her grandmother was seriously ill, and not expected to last the week. She asked if he would grant her paid compassionate leave.

Conferring with Henry Fothergill, Darren found that this was the fifth grandmother that the unfortunate girl was about to lose since she joined the firm. Upon taxing Jenny with this statistic, she explained that her grandfather, a life insurance salesman, recovered quickly from bereavement, and made friends easily: especially to recently bereaved widows with large payouts and poor health. It seemed a pity that he was so unlucky in his choice of life partners. Over lunch one day, Darren relayed this circumstance to Reg Swinton, who immediately resolved to amuse his friend, Detective Sergeant Holmes with the story.

It was about this time when customer complaints started to come in, all relating to incorrectly filled orders. The complaints all had a similar theme, brightly coloured rubber paint sent instead of French polish. Darren immediately suspected Billy. He summoned him to his little wooden cubicle on the loading dock, preparing to give him a serious talking to.

"Top of the morning to you, Mr Darren, sir. You wanted to see me, Mr Darren, sir. Sure it is a grand day today, is it not, sir."

"Yes Billy, but it's not the weather I want to talk about."

"Yes, Mr Darren, Sir. For sure 'tis not just the weather that's grand, if you please. It's a grand place here, and I'm enjoying the work, so I am, Sir. Pat and me bless the day you took us on, Sir. And I hope we are working to your satisfaction, Mr Darren, Sir."

"It's about the work that I want to talk to you, Billy. Some of our customers are complaining about getting the wrong goods. Take this order for example. What does it ask for?"

Darren passed Billy an order form, and waited while the man screwed up his eyes, and mouthed the words on the paper.

"Dat's the French polish, so it is, to be sure, Sir," he said proudly, once he was confident of what he had read.

"And what do you think we sent them?"

"Now dat's a hard one, Mr Darren, Sir. Without the parcel in front of me, I would not like to be guessing dat one."

"How about a half-gallon of pink paint?"

"Now dat can't be right, Mr Darren. What would the customer be doing with the pink paint, if he wanted to French polish a table?"

Darren raised his eyebrows, and waited for Billy to realise that he was implying where the blame rested.

"What sort of an idiot would do dat, Mr Darren, Sir?"

"Have you been making up orders on your own, Billy?"

"Dat I have, to be sure, Sir. Pat has been teaching me the colours, and he's doing a grand job of it at that too, Sir. So he is, to be sure."

Billy reached into his shirt pocket, and brought out a tightly folded sheet of paper.

"Here, dis is what he did," said Billy proudly, as he carefully unfolded the paper. On it was a list of words, mainly names of colours, and against each colour was a little square of paint in the named colour. There were also words like 'paint' and 'polish' with little pictures of the different shaped tins and bottles.

"I'm learning dem fast, Mr Darren, Sir. But if I forget, I just find the word, and look for der little splash of colour on the lid."

Darren was perplexed. Billy was obviously trying hard, and even if he was to blame for the errors, Darren did not have the heart to chastise him.

"Okay, Billy. Get Pat to come and see me, will you."

Darren waited in his booth for Patrick O'Keefe to join him. While he sat there, he watched the team as they brought out made up packages, and stacked them according to their destination. Jenny Wellbeloved ambled out, more slowly than all around her, in a little world of her own, and placed a package on the stack for the van. As she walked away Darren focused on her parcel. It had one of those stick-on fancy bows that you put on gift-wrapped presents, and a pink ribbon instead of parcel tape.

Darren did not have long to dwell on Jenny's packaging technique, as Patrick O'Keefe knocked on his booth door, and opened it.

Without knowing that Darren had asked Billy to send Patrick to him, a casual observer could have assumed that Billy had returned. The twins were identical; until they spoke.

"Good morning, boss. What can I do for you, this cold and frosty morning?"

"I've got a bit of a problem with wrongly filled orders. Are you checking all that Billy does before they are sealed up?"

"I was, but he's not made a mistake in the past three weeks, so I've been a bit lax lately. Besides, I've had him fetching trolley-loads from the stores for the others. How many orders are we talking about?"

"Six in the past week."

Pat shook his head.

"Can't be Billy. I might miss one, but not that many. Can I suggest that you get all the dispatchers to initial the office copy as they complete an order. Then they whose guilt within their bosoms lie, imagine every eye beholds their blame."

Darren nodded. He could have done without the Shakespeare today, and he wished that he had thought of signing off the sheets himself. Until his latest recruits joined him, there had never been a problem, but of course, they had a smaller range of goods as well.

"Okay, Pat. Keep an eye on him, and if it's not him then accept my apologies."

"No harm done, boss. Billy's done well since he's been working for you. It's given him confidence, and I've been encouraging him to read. Only the *Beano* and *Dandy* at the moment, but I plan to move him on to something with fewer pictures soon."

Darren smiled. Just how could the two men be so physically identical, yet so different mentally? He thanked Pat, and sent him on his way. Tomorrow morning he would get all the staff together, and instruct them to sign off orders.

Darren had a restless night. After Pat left, he realised that no matter how he said it, the new instruction would be taken as a way for management to spy on the staff. He had to find a way to dress it up as beneficial to the team, or shift the blame for the new procedure elsewhere.

Next morning Darren stood on the loading bay, and assembled his staff around him. He delivered a little speech about Tracey Mulligan being pleased with how they were coping with the extra work that the new range was generating. He then added his thanks to those allegedly expressed by Tracey, and, almost as an afterthought, added that in line with European Common Market directives they must now initial all orders as they fill them. He explained that it was the only acceptable proof that an order was sent, and protected them individually from complaints about orders lost in the post. Having had his say he asked if anyone had any questions.

"Do we use a pen or pencil?" asked Cuthbert, an elderly long term member of the team.

"Whichever you choose," replied Darren, realising that there was a hidden second question.

"So where do we get the pens?" asked Cuthbert.

Darren smiled.

"I'll go up to Personnel, and get some for those who don't have their own."

With that he made a quick exit, before the discussion turned into a debate about ink colours, pen thickness, and all the other irrelevant minutia that his team could dream up.

After Darren had explained his purpose to Betty in Personnel, she filled in a chit for a dozen ballpoints, and sent him to the accounts office where the stationery cupboard was located. As he walked in, Malcolm from the defunct Wolves supporting production team, was talking to Henry Fothergill.

It had become a tradition in many firms where a few qualified professionals ran teams of manual workers, for those manual workers to seek advice about non-work related problems from those whom they looked on as superior intellects. Today Malcolm was showing Henry a letter he had received from the newly formed Vehicle Licensing Department at Swansea, rejecting his recent form regarding a change of description for an old Ford Prefect.

The car was Malcolm's pride and joy. He had bought it cheaply because it had a damaged roof: the result of a concrete block falling off a passing builder's lorry. He had repaired the roof with Meccano steel plates and fibreglass filler, and then had a bright idea. Recently motor manufacturers were offering an optional extra on some more expensive new cars; a vinyl roof. So Malcolm had asked Potter if he could try out the firm's new rubber paint on the roof of his car. Potter, pleased that the man was showing initiative, and always happy to cite another use for the paint, told him to help himself.

"I don't see a problem there, Malcolm," said Henry, "what are they complaining about?"

"It's the colour names, Mr Fothergill."

"What colour did you use?" asked Henry with deep foreboding.

"*Reeperbahn Red* with *Pleasure Me Purple* imitation stitching."

It was all Henry could do to keep a straight face as he asked his next question. "Why didn't you put the new colour names on the form, the ones we are selling the paint under?"

"That wouldn't have been right, Mr Fothergill. It was old stock from the pilot batches, with the original names on the tins."

"Then I suggest that you submit a new change of colour form. Try *Cherry Red* and simply *Purple* this time."

"You mean I've got to repaint it?"

Henry, almost at the point of giving up, saw that there was only one way to end this idiotic conversation.

"Yes, it will improve the sound deadening, and increase its value when you sell it."

Satisfied with this wise edict from a superior brain to his, Malcolm thanked Henry, and returned to work. He hoped the weather was dry and not too windy over the weekend, now that he had a second paint job to do.

As Malcolm left, Henry made a note to speak to Harry Derry about a special pack aimed at the motorist, with enough paint for a medium sized car roof and a small touch-in tube for mock stitching, but with auto-sport inspired names like *Brands Hatch Blue* and *Brookwood Brown*.

21. BUSINESS BOUNCES BACK

The demand for their rubber paint slowly built up, hastened by advertisements that Harry placed in the new Do-It-Yourself magazines that were beginning to become popular. Retailers of their original products took token stocks of the paint, but they mainly served a rather conservative market. A breakthrough came when Harry succeeded in interesting a national chain of DIY shops in supplying the paints.

Alfred Potter brought a camp bed into the factory in order to run 24-hour production while they built up stocks. It was a double camp bed, and Edith volunteered to provide a basic out-of-hours canteen service for the workers on overtime. During this period of frantic production, most loading and bottling was performed during an extended working day. Potter did little other than monitor and regulate temperatures and pressures within the vast vats during the night hours, but it was a job that needed doing if the vats were to be kept in constant production. Edith accompanied him during this vigil, and saw to his creature comforts between tasks.

In late February, Harry received a phone call from the editor of *Practical Houseowner*, who wanted to do a feature on the product. Harry arranged for him to meet with himself and Alfred Potter one afternoon. A few days later a reporter and photographer from that worthy publication arrived, and spent an hour asking questions and taking photographs.

Eventually a half page article appeared in the magazine, topped by a picture of Harry, sitting poised in his office examining a colour chart. Harry looked decidedly fuzzy in the picture, but in the far background Polly and Susan's mini-skirted legs were sharply focused.

As demand increased, Potter found he could not keep up, even with extended working hours. Additional equipment was brought in and the remains of the Crystal Palace and Charlton supporting polish teams were transferred to paint production. Potter groaned as worker after worker fouled up the simplest of tasks, and eventually took to pasting instruction labels on every conceivable piece of equipment. The factory took on the appearance of a well-annotated museum display, but the incident rate fell, and productivity increased.

Because of his dread of leaving the shop floor unsupervised, Potter brought in an electric kettle, and had his meals sent down to him, so he could keep an eye on the staff while eating.

In line with Potter's philosophy of excessive labelling, his assistant Malcolm thoughtfully marked his mug 'this way up'. Unfortunately, in order to keep the mug still while painting the words, he placed it rim down over one of Edith's rock buns. The resulting words ended up being written backwards. Potter had always regarded Malcolm as one of the more intelligent of the team, and, despite this single act of stupidity, saw much around him to support this belief.

Harry Derry found he was spending a lot of time fielding questions from retailers and customers about potential applications. Long hours, and a job that required much original thinking, were certainly curtailing his home life; much to his, and especially Doreen's, disappointment. Harry approached Tracey with an idea for exhibiting at trade fares and county shows. The idea had one drawback. Neither Harry nor Doreen had a driving licence.

"I used to drive during the war," said Harry.

"In the Merchant Navy?" asked an incredulous Tracey.

"I was sort of lent to the Australians for a while, driving trucks from the meat packing plants to the harbour. I spent three months doing that with a few of the crew after we were sunk off Tasmania… until they declared us fit again and assigned us another ship. I didn't see any point in getting a licence after the war."

"I'll see if I can get John to give you a few lessons. Then if you're happy we'll sort something out."

True to her word, Tracey arranged to get Harry behind the wheel, and with a bit of coaxing he passed his test two months later. Tracey purchased a little Commer van based on the Hillman Imp as a company run-around and Harry set about arranging a schedule of shows and fairs to attend. Most of the county shows were a Friday to Sunday affair, and Doreen enjoyed finding them little country pubs and hotels to stay at for the more distant events.

At work, Harry and Doreen blossomed. With his new skill as a driver they set off most Thursday nights to wherever they had arranged to demonstrate and sell their product. The immediate returns from such events were satisfying, not massive but covering costs, and giving the pair short periods away from the office.

As spring gave way to summer their product range widened, and the programme of demonstrations expanded. Harry and Doreen, decked out in lurid coloured waterproof clothing from the new Peckham Paints workwear range, manned their stall in such exotic locations as Lingfield Racetrack, Catford Dog Track, and Peterborough's East of England showground.

One early summer afternoon at a Sussex show, as a group of Aberdeen Angus cattle were ushered past them on the way to the show ring, Doreen turned to Harry and said something. Harry waited until the noise of bellowing cattle died down before he replied.

"What did you say?"

"Marry me!"

Harry looked at his paramour, and reflected on how the past year had turned life on its head. He had been very content to rub along as they were, with no thought of marriage. He tended to look on Doreen much like an exotic bird, nesting contentedly in his home, but free to fly off should the mood take her.

"Do you really want that? I thought you were happy as we were."

"I was, but now I think it best we get married."

"I don't care much what others think or say. What makes you think we should get spliced?"

Doreen closed upon him, and hugged him. Potential customers strained their ears from the other side of the stall, to hear this impromptu exhibition of elderly romance.

"I didn't want to pressure you, Harry, but it's for the best. I think I'm pregnant."

Harry stood dumbfounded.

"But, But," he spluttered.

"Ashford Decorators Trade Fayre!" she said simply, and he smiled.

The Fayre had a bad first day, with the hall flooded by a burst indoor swimming pool, and they had retired for an early dinner and a long evening in the bar of their hotel. He remembered little else of that night. In the year that Harry had known Doreen, he had assumed that age had protected her from the condition she now proclaimed.

"I know it's bad manners to ask a lady her age," said Harry cautiously, "but if we are to wed, perhaps we should have no secrets."

The few potential customers the other side of the stall had, by now, grown to a tightly packed semicircle that blocked the wide thoroughfare between the two rows of stalls. Privileged beholders at the front relayed the narrative back to the disadvantaged newer joiners at the back. Harry and Doreen, oblivious to their growing audience, stood cuddled together as she whispered a number to him.

The front row, who were by now leaning forward over the stall, and cupping their ears to block out the background sounds of the show, turned and relayed "Fifty two!" to the crowd, drawing a hushed 'Oooooh' from their watchers.

"Yes! I'll marry you. I'll be proud to, if you'll have me," said Harry, and followed his words with a long passionate kiss.

The loud cheer from their audience drew the happy couple's attention for the first time. Harry grinned foolishly, and Doreen blushed deeply. Then they separated, and turned hand in hand to face their audience. A further cheer went up, as others clamoured to join the crowd to see what they were missing.

"Back to work I suppose," she giggled, as she picked up a Peckham Paints *Flower Power* stencil kit, and launched into the product's sales patter about waterproofing tents and baby bibs. Harry stood proudly beside her, lost for words as he slowly took in the full implication of her announcement. If Doreen was right, he could be the only pensioner in Peckham picking up the family allowance on pension day.

The crowd, having been privileged to witness her proposal and announcement, seemed in happy mood, and inclined to hang around. At the end of the demonstration, they cleared the stall of all stencil kits, and much else besides. Perhaps they looked on the cost of their purchases as a form of wedding present to the couple; but for whatever reason Harry and Doreen were left with little to display. They packed up for the night, and sought a telephone, to contact Reg for more supplies.

That evening they retired to bed early, but spent most the night talking. By the morning their initial joy had turned to deep foreboding as reality set in. Whilst Harry had always wanted children, he had not expected to spend his old age bottle-feeding and nappy changing.

For the first time since taking over the company, Tracey felt that things were going the way she wanted them to. Even Henry Fothergill was getting excited about sales figures, as they rose steadily week by week. She had introduced a regular weekly senior managers' breakfast meeting, dubbed Friday Prayers, at which the chosen few discussed new product ideas, and other issues over coffee, bacon rolls and liver sausage sandwiches. Alfred Potter attended and constantly requested more, and bigger, equipment to meet demand for the paint.

Tom Dawes made an observation at one such meeting that the new product seemed to have altered the mind-set of the workers. Almost as if their 18th century product had kept the workforce in that pre-industrial era, and the new paint freed them mentally and encouraged thinking. Not all that thinking was productive, but on the whole they seemed to have a workforce that was growing intellectually.

In the dispatch area, the problem of incorrect orders persisted. Initial attempts to track down the culprit were hampered by workers forgetting to sign off office copies of dispatch sheets. But eventually Darren succeeded in identifying the initials 'JB' as being responsible for all the errors.

Darren was greatly puzzled by this. As far as he knew, he had nobody with those initials on his team. It was a further month before scrutiny of the sheets determined that there were no orders apparently initialled by Jenny Wellbeloved. Upon questioning she declared that her name should be written as 'Jenny Well-Beloved' with a hyphen, and that she did not use the middle initial.

This perplexed Darren even further. He had seen her reading poetry and romantic novels in the canteen, and had no doubts about her ability to understand simple order forms.

"In the past five weeks you have made up seven orders incorrectly," he said accusingly.

"Oh, those! I thought that brighter colours might be better for them than all that dreary brown all the time. They kept asking for the same thing, and I'm sure they were just a bit set in their ways. Are you sure we can't have a blue carpet on the loading bay. It would go so well with the pink lampshades my Granny is crocheting for the lights there."

"You're fired!"

Darren hardly believed what he had just said, and immediately worried that his action might not go down well with the rest of the team. Jenny, however, did not appear to hear him. She was gazing at the floor, and imagining that she was standing ankle deep in sky blue shag-pile.

"Did you hear what I just said? You're fired. You can report to Personnel on Friday, for your wages and P45."

Jenny raised her head, and gazed at Darren.

"Sorry. I was thinking about the carpet. Did you just say that I'm being transferred to Personnel? I'd rather stay here. You're such a lovely person to work for, even if your clothes are a bit dull and old-fashioned."

"Look! If you ever make up an order incorrectly again, you will be fired. DO YOU UNDERSTAND?" he shouted desperately.

Jenny opened her eyes wide, in deep admiration of his masterly tone, then leaped forward, and hugged him.

"I knew you would see it my way eventually. That polish stuff is so old-fashioned. The world should be bright and beautiful, with lots of orange and red and green, not dark brown."

She released him, and scampered away before he could say another word, presumably to miss-fill another order: leaving Darren to speculate about his dull, old-fashioned dress sense, and wonder why he now had a goatskin rug in the booth on the loading dock. Somehow he no longer seemed to be in control of things.

The next morning, whilst Darren was examining the pile of order forms that sales had sent down for the last two hours of the previous day, he heard a gentle cough by his side. He looked up to see a smiling Jenny.

"It's just a little thank you," she simpered, and handed him a soft tissue wrapped parcel.

She smiled shyly as she presented it to him, and then fled to the dispatch room. He opened the package to reveal a broad tie, with such a lurid abstract design that he could use it as a serviette at a barbecue, without significantly altering its eye appeal.

'I wonder if she likes dancing,' Darren wondered idly, as her orange smocked and floral skirted figure disappeared through the swing doors.

He stood reflecting on how managing staff was harder than he would like it to be, and how mixing work with pleasure might not be a good idea. The noise of the swing doors being thrust open brought him back from his musings.

"Ah, Pat! Can I have a word?" he called to his red haired assistant, as the man passed with a stack of three large parcels.

"Begging your pardon, Mr Darren, Sir. Tis meself, Billy. Pat is at the stores with Mr Reg, getting some string. So he is, to be sure, Sir."

Darren smiled. For almost a year the twins had worked for him, and he was still no better at telling which was which. Usually he decided based on the state of the pen clipped to the man's shirt pocket. Billy's generally had a heavily chewed cap, where he gripped it between his teeth as an aid to concentration, whilst he stared at a dispatch form. Darren guessed that he had finally bitten right through, and furnished himself with a new pen. It would be a few days before the familiar dental marks gave Darren the clue he needed to separate them.

"So it is. Morning, Billy. Get Pat to come and see me when he has a moment, would you?"

"Dat I will gladly, Mr Darren, Sir. He'll not be long at all, I tink."

Darren nodded as the eager-to-please Billy stacked his boxes, and ran back through the swing doors to find his brother.

'How long have those doors had flowers painted on them?' Darren wondered as he noticed the yellow, purple and pink flower heads for the first time.

"Greetings, Sir Darren. Thou dist summon me to attend thy bidding this fine morn?"

This time Darren had no doubt who stood in front of him.

"Hello Pat. We need to have a chat. Let's go up to the canteen for a moment."

Pat gave a theatrical bow, and followed Darren towards the stairs.

"A couple of things, Pat. And really I'm just thinking out loud, but I'd welcome your input."

Pat nodded, and took a gulp from the mug of tea Darren had bought him.

"These last few days we've not cleared the early morning orders before lunch. Not the staff's fault, there's just more and more coming in from the sales office after we've finished for the day."

"Overtime?"

"Maybe, but I spoke to the boss, and she says that it is likely that the load will keep increasing. We need to think about a permanent solution, not a stop-gap. We're already doing a full day on Saturday. We never worked a Saturday beyond noon in the old days; and most of that was just tidying up."

"Longer hours? More staff?"

"Something along those lines. But that poses another question. If we were to move to a two shift system, say half come in at eight and the rest at ten, then either I need to be here all the time, or else I need a deputy."

Pat grinned. He could see where the conversation was going, and was pleased that Darren was involving him.

"Suits me," he said presumptuously. "When do you want to start, eight or ten?"

"I'd have to clear it with Miss Mulligan first, but I thought we could do alternate weeks each. And we still need more staff, but the Employment Exchange was useless last time I tried them. Anyone you know who might suit us?"

"Maybe, I'll ask around."

"One last thing, I want to change the way we work. You and me should sort the orders out, and allocate them to the others."

Pat thought back to an earlier conversation they had about Billy's ability to read the dispatch notes.

"You don't have to worry about Billy. He's doing really well. I got him reading *Wind in the Willows* on Sunday, and he hardly had to ask me anything. I had to drag him away to eat his dinner."

Darren smiled at the thought of Billy reading Kenneth Grahame's classic.

"No Pat, It's not Billy, it's Jenny. Try not to allocate her any orders that include French polish. In fact, the brighter the paint colour the better."

Pat frowned, and Darren related his discovery about the incorrect orders, to much amusement and laughing.

"She's in a world of her own, Boss. Did you know that she's got a photo of you in that big hippy shoulder bag she always carries?"

"Me?"

"Yes, a big eight by six glossy. It was taken in the ballroom at the Christmas do. Not a very flattering picture. You're sitting at a table covered in empty glasses, and you've got a somewhat glazed look about you."

Darren thought back, but the latter part of that evening was decidedly fuzzy. He remembered someone standing in front of him, and a camera flash, but little more, other than one of Tom Dawes' foremen escorting him back to his chalet.

"But she's never said anything to me about taking a photograph. She occasionally smiles a bit at me. I'd no idea until recently that she even liked me."

"Maybe not! But I'll tell you another thing. The day you interviewed us, well some of us anyway; she spent the lunchtime buying drinks for Dickie Dickinson and me. Said it was a last leaving drink with the ones she was going to miss working with. It was no accident that Dickie failed to turn up for interview. He must have had at least five doubles, if not more. Mind you, I was none too fit myself by the time we left *The Squinting Badger*. But at least I was on the beer, not spirits."

Darren thought for a moment.

"Just the two of you? Not Winstanton as well?"

Pat shook his head.

"Oswald was a Methodist: no drinking, gambling or swearing. You would not have got him in the pub. I think she was banking on you not taking Billy on. That would have left just three candidates for three jobs."

Pat paused, looking his boss up and down before continuing.

"She definitely has a thing about you, boss... I don't see it myself, but then love looks not with the eyes, but with the mind, and therefore is winged Cupid painted blind."

Darren starred at his empty mug, but it gave no clues as to his fortune or future. So, he thought, Jenny had an obsession about him. She was not bad looking in a Twiggy sort of way, but she always seemed so pre-occupied mentally. Talking to her was like speaking over a very bad telephone connection. Besides that, did he want to encourage someone like her? He had very little success with girls, but he was not sure if the risks might not outweigh the possibilities with Jenny.

"But she never talks to me except about work, and even then she doesn't listen to what I say half the time."

Darren paused to think, perhaps he should have said 'all the time'.

Mary, the canteen assistant, came and collected their empty mugs. She smiled as she took them, and gave the table a quick wipe with a damp dishcloth.

'Nice girl,' thought Darren, but he knew she was engaged to the storesman, and his thoughts drifted back to Jenny. For some reason the thought of her now also brought to mind the Hitchcock film, *Psycho*.

Darren and Pat walked back to the loading bay. As Pat pushed open the swing doors, an unfamiliar smell hit them. There, in a small brass vase atop a stack of parcels, were three smouldering joss sticks.

"Looks like she's moved into the booth, boss."

Darren shook his head in disbelief, but as he did so the door to the booth opened, to reveal a kaftan clad, flower bedecked, Jenny.

"I thought you looked a bit down, so I've made you some Jasmine tea, and a few moon cakes to brighten your aura," she simpered, "and I've got some lovely astra poetry, to help you think beautiful thoughts.

Pat made a quick exit, stifling a giggle until he was safely the other side of the swing doors.

Darren did not really know what his thoughts were at that precise moment. But he was absolutely sure they were anything but beautiful.

22. THE SWEET SMELL OF SUCCESS

Tracey Mulligan became Mrs John Dillon in July, in a quiet ceremony witnessed by just a few family members and a handful of friends, held at Southwark Register Office in Peckham Road. Her aunt, Doreen, was matron of honour in a loose-fitting Mothercare smock and sandals. Doreen and Harry tried their best to look happy for Tracey on this special day, but found it difficult to maintain the required fixed smile. The previous afternoon, Doreen's pregnancy had not only been confirmed, but also she had been given a tentative diagnosis of triplets. As others followed the happy couple out onto the front steps for the traditional photographs, Harry made his way to the administrative office to enquire about free dates for his and Doreen's own official joining together.

Tracey and John's ceremony was followed by a honeymoon tour of the West Country, starting at a hotel recommended by DS Holmes. *The Scrumpydown Hotel* at Collaton had recently changed hands; his lady friend, Milly, now being a part-owner after the previous management found it difficult to run from the confines of Her Majesty's Prisons.

The factory was left in the care of Henry Fothergill and Tom Dawes.

The honeymoon was nearly a non-starter. A paint production worker went missing, with his cap seen floating in a vat of *Passionate Pink*. But he was eventually traced, incarcerated in a lavatory with a faulty lock: his shouts not being heard above the noise of the works.

The success of the rubber paint, however, brought its own problems. With the country booming, it was difficult to recruit staff for the additional production lines that Potter was constantly setting up. Even low levels of sickness required the remaining staff to work overtime to fulfil the ever-increasing orders for the paint.

When the BBC TV children's programme, *Blue Peter,* made a canoe from wire coat hangers and wallpaper, brightly painted in their product to waterproof it, demand went wild. Even in black and white viewing, the programme caught the imagination of children throughout the country, and orders flooded in.

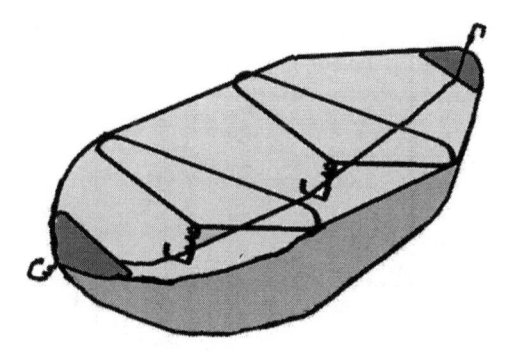

Over the past few days, Darren had succumbed to the hidden charms of Jenny. She made few demands on him, and their romance, if that was the correct word, consisted mainly of her bringing him small gifts of homemade cakes and herbal teas. In return she asked little except the right to sit and gaze at him during lunch breaks, and to read ethereal hippy poetry during their assignations.

She also begged permission to keep and tend the half dozen hanging baskets that hung from the ceiling joists of the loading bay. Darren had hoped that the baskets might add colour to the area, but Jenny was clearly not a successful gardener. All that ever grew there were spiky weeds, but, to her credit, Darren noted that she was most careful to cut them back regularly, and remove the clippings for disposal at home.

This particular morning, Darren was sitting in his booth on the loading bay, eating a batch of cookies that Jenny had brought in for him, when the GPO van arrived. Although physically he was sitting, mentally he was floating a yard above the floor, as he always felt light-headed after a few of Jenny's pungent tasting cookies.

Normally the GPO delivered a couple of dozen orders, and took away perhaps 30 smallish parcels for retail customers. Today the driver approached Darren with a grin on his face. Darren struggled to his feet, and wavered in front of the man.

"Can you get a trolley? I've two sacks of mail for you."

Darren blinked. Recently he had been having problems concentrating, and left a lot of work to Pat. He had also booked an appointment with an optician, as for a week or two things did not seem to be their usual colours, especially from midday onwards. That pink grass on the bombsite opposite, for example, and his green fish and chips last night.

"Two sacks?" he queried, as he stuffed another cookie in his mouth. "What sort of sacks?"

The postman glanced around anxiously for an alternative recipient, preferably someone without glazed eyes who could stand up without swaying. Just then Billy came out of the packing room loaded with parcels.

"Can you get a trolley, young man?" the postman asked. "We've got a lot of mail for you today."

Billy nodded, quickly added his load to an existing stack of parcels, and raced off, to return a few minutes later with the trolley from the stores, and an anxious Reg in pursuit.

Billy assisted the postman in heaving the two bulging sacks up onto the loading dock, and dumped them on the trolley. Darren, meanwhile was focusing on the implications of the delivery, but his mind focused almost as badly as his eyes. He made several attempts to phone the sales office, but failed miserably as the numbers on the telephone dial kept swapping places with each other. Eventually he gave up, and turned to face Billy. His body turned, but his feet remained planted on the floor. As he gyrated round he lost his balance, and retired to a sitting position on the concrete. He looked up with a silly smile on his face.

"We'll have to use the hand lift to get them up to the sales office," he slurred.

Billy nodded, and aimed the trolley at the swing doors, gathering speed as he approached them. Crashing through, he galloped along towards the spot outside the storeroom where a device similar to a domestic dumb waiter was installed. Reg struggled to keep up, as he trailed behind his beloved trolley.

At the hand lift, Billy hoisted a sack in, and turned to Reg.

"If you work dis ting, I'll go upstairs, and take the bags along to dat nice Sandra in sales. Dat I shall, to be sure, Mr Reg, Sir."

With that he was off, running up the stairs two at a time, to await the arrival of the first bag. At that point, Reg found an unexpected problem. He had only ever used the lift to bring goods down. Sending them up was a different matter, as it required considerable time and effort to hoist the heavy container upwards. By the time he had achieved this feat, Billy had returned, wondering why Reg was delaying.

Reg, seeing the man return, assumed that Billy had already unloaded the first bag, and let go of the rope. The lift was a crude device, little more than a box with ropes and pulleys. Darren and Billy watched in horror as it flashed past them to crash to a stop in the basement. Both men dashed down the stairs, into the area where the canteen kitchen used to be. Broken wood and envelopes were strewn over a wide area behind the old serving counter.

Potter, alerted by the noise, summed up the situation quickly, and assigned one of his less useful operatives to assist in clearing up. With the aid of an old biscuit tin, Billy, Reg and the operative ferried batches of letters up to the sales office, where they heaped them in a corner. There was nobody in sales available to accept the post. They were all constantly on the telephone, writing furiously, as orders flooded in from trade customers, who had sold a month's stock in hours.

Billy retrieved the second sack, hoisted it over his shoulder, and again headed for the sales office. Reg retook possession of his trolley. It was slightly before lunchtime.

In the new canteen, the only topic of conversation was the huge demand for their paint that had burst upon them that day. Some, who had watched the *Blue Peter* programme, wondered if they might also be subject to court actions if any child attempted to actually sail their home-made canoe in waters any rougher than a large bath. The programme presenters had demonstrated theirs in a goldfish pond at the BBC's White City Television centre, and for a short period only. At a time prior to the widespread use of video recorders, the programme gave very scant details of how to construct the vessel, and viewers had to rely on their memories, after witnessing a single brief transmission.

Alfred Potter and Tom Dawes sat at a table with Sandra from Sales, trying to assess which colours to produce first to best meet the unexpected demand. Reg joined them, needing to know what sort of packaging materials he needed to order.

23. THE PUNGENT SMELL OF DISORDER

Darren did not dine in the canteen. He was partaking of a candlelit lunch for two, of brown rice and carrot rissoles, in the booth on the loading bay. Over the past week, Jenny had made the booth 'cosy' by the addition of curtains, pictorial beach towels as wall hangings, and a dark blue ceiling embellished with the zodiac in gold and silver. Darren never saw Jenny as she conducted her decorating, but given that the new age foods which she enticed him with were lightly laced with Pot and LSD, he did not notice much else either. Lunchtime seemed to take up most of each hazy day, starting with one or two of Jenny's little cakes with a cup of scented tea about ten o'clock.

He sat on the deeply cushioned two-seater bench that had replaced the chairs in the booth, gazed at their matching embroidered Indian slippers which she insisted he changed into for lunch, and chewed a last mouthful of rice. Jenny slipped her hand inside his unbuttoned flowery shirt, and stroked his relatively hairless chest.

This was his first real physical contact with his hippy assistant, but as a widely read young man, he knew that such things were usually described as a prelude to behaviour which is subsequently declared enjoyable by both parties involved. He slumped back, his head in her lap, and jasmine scent in his head, and prepared to enjoy the experience. As he watched the astral symbols move about the ceiling, talking to each other as they went, he felt wonderful, yet at the back of his mind something was not quite right. He could not remember buying a flowery shirt for a start, and he was sure that he didn't have that tattoo last Christmas. If he had commissioned it himself he would probably have spelt it *'Peace'*, not *'Piece'*. Jenny made herself more comfortable, and started to nibble his ear. He put off thinking about such mundane matters as illiterate tattoos to concentrate on where her hands were going. He did notice that she had locked the door, with a lock he did not, until now, know existed; and she had drawn the thick brocade curtains on the window.

She leaned over him, and blew out the scented candle. In the relative darkness she snuggled down beside him, and continued to nibble his ear.

Piece Man

Darren woke abruptly, woken by Pat hammering on the booth door, and calling his name. Jenny had gone, and the remains of their hippy lunch had been cleared away. He got up carefully, his head fuzzy and his legs not quite steady. He opened the door.

"I'm off now, boss. The GPO have promised to send another van for a further consignment, and both Billy and Cuthbert are staying on to load it. They'll make up as many orders as they can while they wait... And, by the way, I fired Jenny for smoking pot in the packing room. Did I do right, boss?"

"You fired Jenny?"

"Yes, boss. I spoke to Mr Fothergill first. And since you were incapacitated at the time, he said I should go ahead and fire her."

Darren shook his head, but it did nothing to clear it. Pat interpreted the act as disapproval and began to object.

"Wait! Give me time to think. How did you know she was smoking pot?"

"She had a big ornamental pipe, puffing away, and she was behaving really weird. She had an order to fill, but we had run out of the bigger boxes it needed, so she addressed a smaller box, opened a tin and poured the paint into it. You should have seen the mess."

Pat looked back at the trails of orange footprints that criss-crossed the bay, before continuing.

"Mind you, I can't be absolutely sure that was what happened. With the smoke from that pipe, we were all starting to see things that weren't really there. Cuthbert told me his mother was coming to dinner tonight, and I know for a fact that she was killed during the war when the Germans bombed Woolworths in New Cross."

"But why didn't anybody come and find me?"

"We tried to, boss, but you were out cold. I think she's been doping you somehow. I did warn you she was trouble."

"Yes, yes. You did right, Pat. But did she take any notice of you? I've tried to fire her twice before, and she just heard what she wanted to."

"I'm not sure, boss. But, while I was talking to her, Reg from the stores came in. He took one sniff, and made a phone call. A detective and a uniformed copper turned up a few minutes later, and took her away... I never knew he had so much influence. It took an hour to get a policeman when Billy was set upon by two muggers, by which time he had flattened the pair of them, and had to stand in the rain, with his feet on their hands, while he waited."

Darren closed his eyes, and sat down. Standing had been an effort, and there were strange animals running about behind Pat. Come to think about it, Pat never used to have blue hair, or a tail.

"I think you need to see a doctor, boss. Shall I get Mr Fothergill to call the company Doc?"

Darren thought for a moment, at least to him it seemed like a moment, but to Pat it was an eternity, so he made his own decision.

"I'll get Billy to come and sit with you. I shan't be a minute."

Pat sped away, and soon his twin came to keep their befuddled boss company. Darren was not sure why Pat had a yellow and green striped elephant sitting with him, even if it did have a voice like his brother.

After a while, Darren saw a van approach, and struggled to his feet to help load it. He watched the van change colour, and size, several times while Billy and Pat escorted him to what was, in fact, an ambulance.

After hearing Pat's description of Darren, the company doctor decided that Darren would be safer out of the public eye until his body had disposed of all trace of unwanted substances. So he had arranged for him to have a short stay in St Borgia's. Darren could look forward to a five-day detoxification diet consisting of nothing except weak lemon juice, and regular coffee enemas, before he was reassessed for further treatment.

The huge demand for paint products subsided after a few days; back closer to the steady volume that it had achieved before the BBC created their DIY vessel. Potter breathed a sigh of relief, and took the rare step of leaving the factory for an hour or so each evening. Normally this was in the company of Edith, and usually the pair returned reeking of garlic and curry in an amorous mood, which necessitated them to retire to the privacy of the canteen's dry goods stock room.

To facilitate these recuperative periods, Edith had ordered a stock of twelve 56 lb sacks of haricot beans, which served as makeshift furniture for the couple. Subsequently neck of lamb stew with mashed haricots, and bean soup made regular appearances on the canteen menu.

Darren did not return to work for almost a fortnight, by which time he had been twice visited by the local police, who had also been to the factory to confiscate the hanging baskets from the loading area. Detective Sergeant Holmes made the second visit, during which he lectured Darren about his stupidity, and informed him that both Jenny and her grandfather were currently guests of Her Majesty: the former for possession of drugs, and the latter as a result of an exhumation of a recently departed step-grandmother. It was only Holmes' gratitude to Tracey for many useful leads that saved the witless Darren from charges.

Upon his return, Darren looked fit and well, but thinner. He was inclined to prefer to stand while working. A week of four coffee enemas a day had left him decidedly uncomfortable in the sitting department. He had also developed an aversion to small cakes, especially those of a dark colouring.

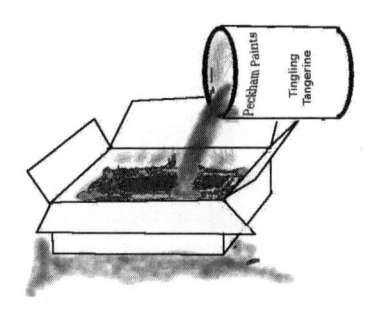

24. PAINTING THE TOWN RED

Malcolm woke for another day at work, and looked out of his bedroom window, squinting in the bright sunshine as he surveyed the dusty baked earth and wilting shrubbery. It was late August and there had been almost no rain since Easter - but it was not the garden or the weather that Malcolm was looking at; he was watching for the cluster of people who tended to congregate around his car. He was, in his own opinion, a bit of an artist, and with careful brush strokes had created a very passable vinyl effect on the roof of the Ford. When he had chosen the bright red, he had no idea how eye-catching it would be, contrasting with the cream of the remaining paintwork. He got so many comments and queries from passers-by that in the end he started carrying a pack of company sales literature in the boot, with a data sheet taped to the rear window.

A friend, the owner of an elderly Morris Traveller, had asked him if he would do a similar job on his car, and soon a second person made the same request. As the weeks went on, several others approached him, and Saturday afternoons became a profitable sideline. He also started to notice other red-roofed vehicles around Peckham, and begrudged the competition. Like the Lambretta of the early sixties, having a red roofed car would appear to have achieved cult status in Peckham. It did not seem to matter how incongruous the colour was to the remainder of the vehicle, the roof simply had to be red rubber.

Today Malcolm saw two men standing admiring his Ford Prefect, whilst a slim woman of about forty was actually stroking the vehicle, much as you might a pet cat. He dressed hurriedly, and decided to have breakfast at work. He pulled his front door shut with a bang, to announce his presence, and sauntered casually up the footpath to the roadway. Once he was there, he fished in his pocket for his keys, before looking up in mock surprise at his car's admirers.

"Good morning. Lovely day again."

Both men verbally concurred about the weather, but the woman only smiled. The group did not look like the usual boy-racers who congregated beside the distinctively painted vehicle, and Malcolm wondered about their interest. Having got their attention, he enquired innocently, "Can I help you?"

The older of the two men cocked his head on one side, and surveyed Malcolm carefully. It was a practised eye, skilled at summing up a person in a single glance, usually before offering his professional services.

"Did you do this?" he asked, gesturing at the car's roof.

"Yes," replied Malcolm proudly. "I work for Peckham Paints."

"And did you also do that Daimler over there?"

The tone of the man's voice implied that it would not be in Malcolm's best interest to admit to the task, even if he had performed it.

"Daimler? No, certainly not," retorted Malcolm, as he scanned along the road until he saw a limousine that looked as if it had been painted with the wrong end of a toothbrush. "That's a dreadful job, and the person who did it should be shot."

"So he will be when I find him. I've got six of them like that, and it will cost me a fortune to get it put right."

Malcolm, slow witted as he was, began to sense a problem.

"Are you saying that someone painted them without you knowing?"

The younger of the two men turned from the car to face Malcolm. He was a rather insipid looking late-twenties, in a charcoal grey suit.

"They were all lined up ready for a funeral. Polished and cleaned inside, sparkling they was. I went in for dinner, and they were like it when I came back out."

"In broad daylight?"

"Yes!" he replied vehemently.

"Have you contacted the police?"

"Of course I have!" he replied indignantly, "But they don't have a clue."

Malcolm thought for a bit, then smiled.

"Six of them? That would take quite a bit of paint. I tell you what I'll do. I'll have a word with our sales people. See if we can pin down that amount of red to a local order. Can I have a closer look?"

Without waiting for permission, he ambled across the road and peered closely at the car roof.

'Hmm. They tried to do imitation stitching in Seductive Green. What have we got here?' he wondered, as he focused on a mark in the paint. Malcolm turned to the two men and the woman, who had followed him.

"Did the police take this fingerprint?"

Three heads shook in unison.

"I'll have a word with our storeman. He seems to have contacts in the police. You'd better give me your address, so I can get back to you."

The older man reached into his waistcoat pocket for a business card.

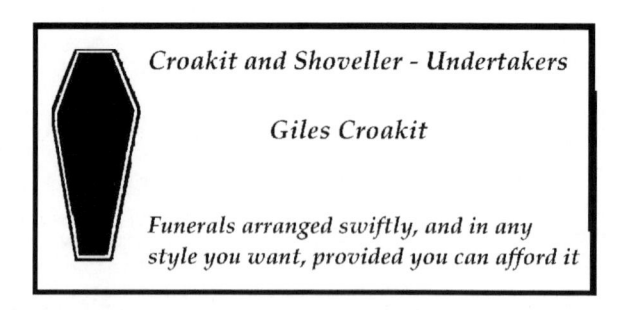

Croakit and Shoveller - Undertakers

Giles Croakit

Funerals arranged swiftly, and in any style you want, provided you can afford it

---

He wrote a phone number on the back, and handed it to Malcolm.

"We are available any time," he said, as he eyed Malcolm up again with that professional look. "My associate, Mr Shoveller here normally answers during office hours, and I at other times. Good day."

Malcolm took the card and smiled, but inside he felt like anything except smiling. The man was clearly sizing him up for a final resting place: one he was not ready for.

"I'll give you a call in a few days," he said, wondering about the woman, who had maintained her silence so far.

As the little group left, she turned and winked at him. It was a rather conspiratorial wink, as if he and she shared a secret that no one else was to be party to.

At the factory, Malcolm briefly told Potter about his conversation with the little group. Potter went pale as Malcolm spoke of the woman.

"The woman! Slim brunette, with a gold amulet on her right wrist?"

Malcolm thought for a while. He pictured her stroking the roof of the car, the sun glinting on gold as she did so.

"Yes. Do you know her?"

Potter, already quite pale, went white.

"My wife!"

Malcolm stood silently for a moment, then raised his eyes upward towards the upstairs canteen. He did not need words to comment on Potter's and Edith's relationship.

"It's a long story. She ran off with a surgical appliance salesman in the late fifties, but just occasionally she makes contact. I heard she had taken up with an undertaker. I thought they were up north somewhere."

Malcolm fished out the card, and examined the back of it. It was a local number. He showed it to Potter.

"Oh, well. Can't be helped. Did she mention me?"

"No. In fact she didn't say a word. I wasn't even sure she could speak."

"Oh! Goodness! I thought she might be cured of that by now. It's that shade of red. It makes her go quite odd. She named it for me when I first went into production. It always got her passions going, and once aroused, she would always be silent until her longings were satisfied, apart from the occasional moaning sound."

Potter's voice softened as he spoke, and he stood dreamily reminiscing about his estranged wife's peculiar behaviour.

Malcolm frowned, and wondered which of the two men she was with. Surely not the older of the two, yet the younger one did not seem the sort to invoke or satisfy passions. Maybe their profession made them mask their emotions in public.

After some debate about the vandalism Potter agreed that having some maniac going round slapping paint on cars was not going to be good for business. He sent Malcolm off to see Reg, while he went upstairs to find Henry Fothergill.

"Morning Alfred. What can I do for you?"

"Young Malcolm has stumbled on a problem. Someone is going round putting our paint on car roofs. I'm just off to Sales to see if anyone had bought *Reeperbahn Red* and *Seductive Green* together."

"*Cherry Red* and *Apple Green*?"

Potter nodded. Henry was a stickler for using the public names for the shades, whilst most of Potter's production team still used his original lurid descriptions. But Henry was curious.

"Tell me Alfred, why *Seductive Green*?"

"No idea, contrasts with the red, perhaps. I wouldn't have used that for stitching myself."

"No. I mean why did you call it *Seductive Green*? Green's not known for its seductiveness."

"She had red hair and green eyes, like a cat," replied Potter, "I was still at college, and she worked in the sweetshop down the road from my lodgings. She used to give me extra wine gums, then one day she invited me to see her cherry bonbons in the stock room."

He drifted off, into a dream of hot sweaty summer afternoons in the back room of the little shop.

"So you'll speak to Sales," said Henry, in an attempt to focus Potter's mind on the present.

Enquiries in the sales office did not help Potter. Sandra went through a month's orders, and nowhere did anyone buy a large quantity of the red together with some green, except a firm in Skegness. Certainly no obvious local candidates.

Malcolm got no real success with Reg either. Reg phoned his friend DS Holmes. Holmes had heard of the incident, but was equally puzzled. A typical vandal would have attacked one vehicle, and fled before discovery. He suspected someone with a grudge against the undertakers, rather than something that might become a trend. They had only recently set up in the area, and he was concentrating his enquiries on the less respectable of their rivals. Reg wondered what an un-respectable undertaker looked like. Burke and Hare perhaps?

Reg mentioned the fingerprint that Malcolm had spotted, and Holmes promised to investigate. He phoned back later to say that he could not find it, but there was now an area on the car roof where the paint had been scratched off.

That evening, Malcolm drove home, the incident still in his mind. He locked the car, and absent-mindedly walked up the path to his front door. There, sitting on the doorstep and hidden from the road by a hydrangea, was the woman. He nodded and greeted her, but she made no reply. Potter's words came vividly back to him. He looked round cautiously, then unlocked the door. She got up, glanced back along the path to where he had parked the Ford, and followed him silently into the house. It was almost midnight before she spoke to an exhausted Malcolm!

"Please don't spend too much time trying to find who painted our cars. I'm sure you have better things to do with your time."

Malcolm grunted. She had regained her voice but he was too short of breath to speak. There was something in the way she spoke that suggested that she might be willing to assist him in finding better ways to fill his time... and he was sure he would be very happy to accept such assistance.

Next morning, he woke to find her standing and gazing out of the bedroom window at his car, especially the roof. He bid her a good morning, but got no reply. She simply turned, smiled and walked back towards him.

It was nearly noon before a weary Malcolm arrived at work. In his heart he suspected that the woman may know much more about the painted funeral cars than she was prepared to say. He kept his suspicions to himself, and picked up a tin of *Reeperbahn Red* to paint his front door and bathroom walls with.

Malcolm's experience with the woman was repeated twice that week. On the Friday evening, a few minutes before eleven, the woman smiled, and prepared to leave his house.

"I can't stay tonight. I've got to be at our Skegness office in the morning. I'll be back in a week, but before I go, what's your telephone number?"

As he quietly closed the front door behind her, he realised she had still not told him her name. He longed to know it, but common sense had prevented him from asking Potter what his wife's first name was.

On the following Thursday, Potter showed Malcolm that week's Peckham Echo. On page two was an article about an undertaker who had opened a branch locally, but who had decided to sell up after a number of incidents. There was a quote from a Mr Giles Croakit, below a picture of a pair of paint-splattered hearses.

"We've been in business for twenty years, and have six branches in Lincolnshire and Humberside but never have we met such wanton vandalism as in this last month in London."

Malcolm gazed at the paper, and wondered if he would ever see the woman again.

"Mr Potter," he asked cautiously, "where did your wife come from originally?"

"Cleethorpes, on the East Coast. She never did like living in London. She found the air here oppressive after the North Sea breezes. I suspect that was part of why she ran off. Why do you ask?"

"No reason," mumbled Malcolm, as he folded the paper and put it down on the bench. He wondered how long it took to drive to Skegness, and if it was practical to do so over a weekend.

25. PITFALLS IN THE COURSE OF LOVE

August rolled into September, and the new Mrs Tracey Dillon returned to take up control of her factory. Much to her surprise, the place had flourished in her absence. There were two new redheaded assistants in dispatch, an enlarged paint production line in the old canteen, and two-shift working on the presses stamping out their various stencil kits. The foremen and charge hands had thrown off their outdated mind-sets, and adopted a more flexible approach to work, which included unplanned overtime as appropriate and multi-tasking. Whether this indicated an awareness of the need to be profitable, or simply a desire to curry favour with their boss, was not clear.

Henry Fothergill had extended his interest from counting the money to innovating the product range. To this end he had co-opted his elder daughter to design a range of stencils, to extend their appeal from the flower people to the public at large. Although designed for use with their rubber paints, they caught the public imagination and sold in great numbers at the exhibitions and agricultural shows. Harry and Doreen imagined Roman friezes and Victorian motifs adorning the walls of cowsheds and milking parlours, as they sold set after set to tweed clan farmers.

Sometimes twins run in families, and this was certainly true of the O'Keefe clan. Moira and Lisa O'Keefe were cousins of Patrick and William, who had been encouraged to come to London to seek their fortune in the entertainment industry. It was only after arriving that they found the promised 'opening into the entertainment world' was in fact the doorway of a seedy Soho clip joint where they were expected to stand scantily clad, and lure customers in. Too ashamed to return home to their native land, they had sought help from their cousin Patrick. Pat immediately introduced them to Darren, with the intention of getting them employment in the factory.

Darren, after talking to the young women, and finding that educationally they more closely resembled Pat than Billy, had no hesitation in taking them on. He only really needed one extra member of staff, but like Billy and Pat, the girls were inseparable so it was both or neither.

Two pairs of identical twins proved a challenge to Darren, for both girls had very similar voices, and he struggled to identify who he was speaking to at any one time. But, by the end of a fortnight or so, he worked out that Moira always wore big gold earrings, whilst Lisa had a silver Celtic cross on a short leather lace around her neck.

One of the aspects of employing numerous members of one family is that their social life has a tendency to impact on work. Darren feared he could lose half his workforce for a funeral, although to his relief he found they only possessed a normal number of grandparents: and those were apparently hale and hearty farming stock who sent regular parcels of produce to their city-bound grandchildren. The girls were of a generous nature, and often shared their good fortune with their workmates, an act which quickly made them popular with their co-workers.

Over the period of the following month, Darren became friendly with Lisa, and he hoped that she was not adverse to himself. Certainly her smile broadened when she saw him, and she would stand fingering her Celtic pendant as he gave her instructions to carry out.

As is often the case with twins, one is bolder than the other. Lisa was the shy one, and she awoke the protective instinct in Darren, in a way that her more outgoing sister did not. Darren was very aware that Pat was also protective of his cousins, and was cautious of approaching Lisa to ask her out on a date. Instead he suggested that he, Pat, Billy, the two girls and his brother, Brian, went dancing one evening at the Rivoli Ballroom in Crofton Park. It was two short stops on the train from Peckham Rye station, set in a mainly residential area with a few shops around it.

The evening did not go quite as Darren had hoped. They arrived early whilst the ballroom was still sparsely populated, and sat in the bar for a drink before approaching the dance floor. Once there, Darren lost no time in asking Lisa to dance, and was soon skilfully guiding her round the polished floor. Patrick partnered Moira for a less skilful, but reasonably competent twirl around.

Billy stood surveying the other occupants, ready to smile at any young lady who returned his glance. Eventually he made eye contact with a smiling auburn haired girl in a blue dress, and returned her smile whilst crossing the floor towards her. He stood in front of where she sat, and introduced himself. As he extended his hand, and asked her if she would like to dance, he became aware of a voice behind him.

"What do you think you're doing?"

Billy turned, focusing his smile to the crewcut young man standing behind him with two drinks in his hands.

"Good day to yourself, Sir. I was just about to ask dis young lady if she would oblige me with a dance."

"Piss off, Paddy. She's with me."

"Now den Sir, dats no way to speak in front of a lady. And der's no cause to be offensive, Sir. Good day to you, Sir, Miss."

With that Billy stepped sideways to pass Crewcut and re-cross the floor. There was an occupied table and chairs to his right, and Billy held his arm forward in a gesture commonly used to request passage in crowded spaces. Crewcut interpreted this as a threat, and threw both drinks at Billy.

"Now der's no cause…"

But Billy did not complete the sentence, as Crewcut dumped the empty glasses on a table, and aimed a blow at his face. It was foolish behaviour on the part of the Crewcut. Billy outweighed him by more than two stone, and every ounce of that weight advantage was made up of hard muscle. He fended off the man's puny blow, and numerous others for some time before becoming bored, and laying him out with a single punch which probably broke the man's jaw.

At this point others, who claimed friendship with the man, joined in, and Pat quickly raced across the floor to offer support to the outnumbered Billy. Darren, sizing up the situation, and deciding that retreat was a sensible option, tried to usher Lisa and Moira away towards the exit. Brian joined them, and, taking Lisa by the arm, steered her away.

But Moira was not one to abandon her benevolent cousins in their hour of need. Picking up a chromed metal barstool, she waded into the conflict like a battle-axe wielding Viking warrior, twirling the stool around her head, and picking off three assailants before they were aware of her entry into the combat. Faced with three such formidable opponents, many of those present decided that they did not know young Crewcut so well after all, and that they had more pressing business elsewhere. The auburn-haired girl melted away into the crowd.

Someone must have phoned the police, because a distant two-tone horn was heard to approach. Darren looked round for Brian and Lisa, but they were already outside, so he called to Pat to get Billy and Moira to follow him. A hasty retreat saw the six regroup on the pavement outside, and a quick walk to the nearest side road away from the hall. In the relative gloom and quiet of a residential street, they considered their options. As a group they were easy to describe, with two pairs of identical twins present. So the decision was made to split up. Brian, who was still standing close to Lisa, went off with her down Beecroft Road, and Darren found himself walking with Moira. Billy and Pat separated, to make their way home singly.

The skirmish seemed to have aroused Moira. Her face was flushed, she was breathing heavily, and in the quiet street her earrings seemed to jangle and clank like the warning bell of a medieval leper. She clung to Darren's arm, and set the pace as they walked through empty residential streets. Despite the cool air and the monotony of the landscape, she chattered on, still in a heightened state of alertness after her brief spell of activity. When they reached a little parade of shops, she dragged Darren sideways into the darkness of a shop doorway for a long passionate snog. Eventually her heaving breast subsided to a calmer state and, prompted by the smell of vinegar and frying wafting on the air from a few doors down, more basic needs took over. The excitement of the evening had rapidly depleted her energy levels, and she required rock and chips, with two pickled onions and a gherkin, to restore her.

After satisfying her hunger, Moira returned to her more normal self, sedately walking hand in hand with Darren, and leading the conversation. There was still a good twenty-minute walk home, during which Darren began to worry about how Brian and Lisa were progressing. He earnestly hoped that any progress was purely perambulatory, without detour into shop doorways en-route.

Eventually they arrived at the house Moira shared with her twin and cousins. She turned to Darren, thanked him enthusiastically for a wonderful evening, and planted a final long, full lipped, onion flavoured kiss on his lips, before disappearing indoors.

Darren stood on the pavement, bewildered by her behaviour. It was as if she thought the events of the evening were normal, even essential, ingredients of a good night out. He headed home, where he found that, much to his relief, Brian had arrived twenty minutes earlier, and had already retired for the night.

'Obviously no time for detours, or extra-perambulatory activity on the way,' thought a relieved Darren, as he ascended the stairs to bed.

The next day dawned bright, and Darren anticipated another normal day's work at the factory. As his team arrived there was little evidence of their night out, unless you looked hard to see the slight swelling of Billy's lower lip. But things were not normal. Lisa refused to speak to him, clearly going out of her way to avoid her boss whenever possible, whilst Moira made any trivial excuse she could to ask him about orders and packaging. Moira accompanied her conversations with smiles, as much bodily contact as circumstances allowed, and with blown kisses as she took her leave back through the swing doors to the packing area.

Darren was totally bemused by her, and was relieved to find that both Billy and Pat seemed to be their usual selves. It was a hectic day and not until late afternoon did Darren find time to take a break in the canteen. He was halfway through a mug of tea when Pat sat down beside him.

"That was a bit of a lively evening last night, boss. Not quite what I expected, what with Billy not getting home until two. And you're full of surprises, yourself."

"Yes, I don't think we'll be going there again in a hurry."

"I wasn't thinking about the dance hall. I was thinking about you and Moira. I always thought it was Lisa that you fancied."

"What do you mean, me and Moira?"

"Come on, boss. Your secret's safe with us. She told us all about it when she got home."

"About what?"

"How you and she... well, you know."

"You mean how she dragged me into the doorway of the Co-op, and did an imitation of an octopus in a breath-holding competition?"

"That's not the way she tells it. She said you planned it all, right from the start. What with holding hands, choosing the darkest streets to walk down, and suchlike. Then later you bought her supper, and sat on a wall while you told her how much you cared for her."

"What? I did no such thing! Yes, I bought her fish and chips, but only because she said she was hungry after all that activity. And the only reference I made to caring was about not getting chip fat on her dress."

"What activity?" demanded Pat, his voice more terse now that there was a suggestion that his kinswoman's honour might be in question.

"In the Rivoli, and walking home," replied Darren defensively.

Pat ignored the first part of Darren's answer, focusing on the 'activity whilst walking home' element.

"So you admit that you and she stopped somewhere, before you got to the chip shop?"

"Yes, but it was Moira who did the stopping. One moment I was walking by the kerb, and the next she had dragged me into the doorway. I opened my mouth to protest, and found I had two tongues in it."

"And you didn't give her a present. A token of your affection, as it were?"

"No. The only thing I gave her was an old hanky to rest her supper on, to save spoiling her dress. She wiped her greasy hands and face on it too, once we'd finished eating."

"A hanky? A white handkerchief with your initials on it, for her to put under her pillow, and induce dreams of you?"

Darren gulped as he remembered that instead of returning the cloth, she had put it in her handbag. At the time he assumed that she might wash and return it.

"No. It was just an old hanky that I got for Christmas one year."

"And you didn't say anything about her looking good in a white dress?"

Darren squirmed as he analysed the numerous interpretations that his simple compliment could have.

"Well she did; she looked lovely. Just like Lisa would have done sitting there."

Pat frowned, and then laughed.

"The way Moira tells it, boss, is that you were hinting about how she would look in a wedding dress. As if you were sounding out her feelings for you. She kept us up half the night telling us how passionate you were, and how you virtually proposed. That's how we know what time Billy returned. Lisa was in tears."

"The only thing I proposed was to find a chip shop... Why was Lisa in tears?"

"Because, until last night she fancied you, you daft pillock."

Darren and Pat sat silently for a while. Darren reflected on the fact that it seemed to be his fate to attract unwanted admirers, whilst somehow, through no fault of his own, spoiling his chances with the girl he desired.

"Can't you tell Lisa the truth for me, Pat?" he asked miserably.

"Okay, Boss. I'll do my best, but she might not believe me. She and Moira are very close you know, and Moira has the handkerchief as evidence of your affection... Besides, I'm not sure how you can convince Moira that you did not have feelings for her, not after she's made her mind up. I think she spent lunchtime in Jones & Higgins bridal department."

Darren went pale.

"I think I'll go home early. I don't feel too well."

"Okay, Boss. Do you want me to tell Moira. She makes a good chicken soup, and is probably itching to come round, and look after you."

Darren opened his mouth to speak, but Pat burst out laughing before his bewildered brain could find anything appropriate to say.

"Don't worry Boss. I'll look after things, and see what I can do to sort it all out."

That evening, Darren had a redheaded visitor. He breathed a sigh of relief as he noted the absence of earrings, and the gleam as the light shone on the little silver cross at her throat. She stepped shyly across the threshold, and hugged him gently. Darren led her to the front parlour, and then went to make coffee.

They spent the evening listening to records, and talking a little about their very different upbringings: he in London, and she in a small village near Cork. They made no mention of the previous evening, except to speculate on why Billy was so late home. Darren silently thanked Patrick for whatever he had said to sort out the misunderstanding. As the evening progressed, they cuddled and kissed, before planning more intimate explorations.

As Darren ventured to undo a top button on her blouse, she pushed him away gently.

"Wait a minute, while I take this cross off," she said softly. "Lisa will kill me if I break it for her. She doesn't know I've borrowed it."

26. GERIATRIC GESTATION

Next day, Darren dreaded going to work. He had spent the previous evening pouring his soul out to Moira, whilst believing that it was Lisa in his arms. If he had started the previous day in a mess, then today he had a full sized intercontinental disaster. Moira had gone home in a bad mood after he had switched from passionate to irate, but not until she had pointed out how pleased he had been when she arrived, and how eager he had been for the first part of the evening.

It was a difficult day for Darren. Moira would not speak to him because of his attitude once he realised he had spent the evening with her. Lisa would not speak to him because he had spent the evening with Moira, and neither girl would speak to each other either.

Darren used Pat and Billy as go-betweens to pass work instructions, and the day jogged uncomfortably along. At about three o'clock, news filtered down to the loading bay that an ambulance had been seen outside the factory, and later details circulated describing Doreen Mulligan being taken to King's College Hospital. The news seemed to put squabbles on the loading area into perspective, and the various workers began to begrudgingly speak to each other. This did not completely solve Darren's social problems. Neither O'Keefe girl was wearing earrings or a crucifix today.

In the stores, Reg heard the news about Doreen, and immediately went up to the management office suite to find more details. Harry had gone with the ambulance, and Tracey had left half an hour later to join him at the hospital. Susan and Polly had little information other than it was related to Doreen's pregnancy. Reg made his way to the canteen, where Edith and Mary were tidying up prior to leaving for the day.

"I'll get the train over to Denmark Hill, and see what's going on, then either come home or phone you," said Mary reassuringly.

Reg nodded, kissed her, and went back to the stores. His two assistants were relabelling the tins of paint that they had incorrectly labelled in the morning, and he had stock reports to correct before he could leave.

Reg had known Harry for three years, and Doreen for two. They were almost family to him. Since his mother was still in Spain, he only had Harry, Doreen and Mary whom he considered close to him. He was pleased when five o'clock struck, and he could clock out.

Reg walked home slowly, climbing the five flights of stairs to the flat in a dream. As he neared his front door he heard a phone ring in the distance. He rushed to open the door, but the sound was no louder inside. He automatically switched the electric kettle on, and stood watching it as it came to the boil.

Reg was dozing in front of the television when the phone eventually rang. He woke drowsily and picked up the receiver.

"Hello!"

"Reg, it's all right. Doreen had a problem, but is okay. They are keeping her in for a day or so, to check on her. Tracey asked if we would like to go to dinner with her and John. I'll see you there."

She hung up, and Reg looked at the clock. It was almost seven. As he stood up to change before going out, he suddenly realised that Mary had not specified where they were having dinner. It could be either the new town house that Tracey and John had bought at Honor Oak, or the Indian restaurant opposite the cinema. After an agonising ten minutes he decided that Mary meant Tracey's home, and set off into the autumn evening.

The relative newly-weds, John and Tracey, had bought a new, split-level, house built on a steep hill at Honor Oak. As the post-war development boom scoured the country for building plots, a number of previously uneconomic sites had been built on, and this was one. The house was part cut into the hill, and part projected out above ground level, and with its several adjacent kin, stood out from the more traditional architecture of the older houses on the flatter sections of the road. It had a neat lawn, and small newly planted shrubs and roses marking the frontage. Next door had no curtains, a partly turfed lawn and a small pile of builder's rubbish out front, and the further three new houses were clearly still not quite complete.

Reg was relieved to see Dillon's Morris Oxford parked in the driveway, and pressed the doorbell button in anticipation of a pleasant evening with friends.

There was no response to his first ring, and a feeling of foreboding set in. A second press was also in vain, and Reg silently cursed. As he turned away, anticipating a walk back to Peckham, and a belated reunion with Mary at *The Star of The East*, a taxi drew up. Tracey, Harry and Mary alighted and approached.

"Been here long?"

"Just arrived. How is Doreen?"

"After I spoke to you, the doctor decided that it would be safer for all if she had a caesarean. The poor little mites are okay, but will need to stay in hospital for a while. Not one was over four pounds."

"And Doreen?"

"Sleeping off the anaesthetic, but it all went well."

"What are they?"

"Three girls."

Tracey unlocked as Mary filled in the details for Reg, and they went up to the first floor, where the lounge and kitchen were located.

"I thought John would be in, as his car is outside."

"Oh, that's for sale. We treated ourselves to a new car a couple of weeks after we got back from honeymoon. I found I was getting backache on long journeys while we were away."

She giggled! A giggle that told Reg that there was more to the story than she had so far told him. Reg frowned. He had often been driven about in the Morris, and found it very comfortable. Tracey giggled again, and whispered something to Mary.

"Oh, I'm sure Reg can keep a secret," said Mary, and joined Tracey in her giggle.

"Tracey's expecting," said Mary.

"Expecting what... Oh! When?"

"Next February!"

Dinner was a hastily cobbled together meal: heavily reliant on the new chest freezer in the downstairs utility room, and eaten on trays while sitting in the lounge. Whilst daylight lasted it was a pleasant way to eat, with an elevated view out over woodland behind them, and as darkness fell, the lights of the town gave them a feeling of being above, and detached from, the noise of suburban London.

The talk was mainly about maternity and motherhood. Reg felt that he was out of his depth, unable to make any real contribution to the conversation.

As the evening wore on, Mary kept looking across at him, and smiling. Although he and she had announced their engagement last Christmas, they had got no further in planning a wedding date. This was partly because both were happy with things as they were, the engagement being to declare their exclusivity to each other, and partly because they agreed that they would like to save their money and seek somewhere better to live, before naming the day.

Reg had possessed money, some four thousand pounds of Ernshaw's, which he was supposed to use in pursuance of Big Ernie's criminal empire, but he never considered it his own, and had loaned it to Tracey to help pay off the cost of buying the company. Currently he and Mary were saving towards a deposit on a house, and spent most of their weekends viewing property. Anything they saw that was remotely within their estimated price range made depressing viewing.

"Reg, you've got a driving licence, haven't you?" asked Tracey.

"Yes."

"Well, the Morris is just sitting there, so if you and Mary want to borrow it at any time you are most welcome."

Reg smiled as he recalled the circumstances of him acquiring a driving licence. He had barely an hour driving round in one of Ernshaw's getaway vans, and then a driving test taken for him by one of Ernshaw's drivers.

"I think I'd need a bit of practice before I drove anything on my own again," he said modestly, as he remembered the incident with the vicar's bicycle when he 'borrowed' a van from a neighbour. It all seemed so long ago now, almost as if it had happened to a different person.

John Dillon arrived while Tracey's visitors were getting ready to leave. The car he parked on the drive was like nothing Reg had ever seen before: long, sleek and futuristic looking, more like an aircraft in its styling. As Reg scanned the bodywork for a badge or word he would recognise, the vehicle gave a little sigh, and settled lower to the ground. He looked round in alarm, but John stood behind him and was clearly not concerned.

"Just shutting down the hydraulics," said John.

"What is it?"

"Citroen GS. Most comfortable car in the world. We bought it because the Morris was giving Tracey backache on long journeys. If we'd waited a week, we would have known that the backache was caused by pregnancy, not the car. But never mind, it's lovely to drive... And no backache! They wouldn't part-exchange the Morris, as it's too old."

Reg and Mary walked as far as Nunhead with Harry. It was only a little out of their way, and they felt he might like the company. Harry, himself, was having difficulty defining his current mood. He was elated, and terrified at the same time, about the birth of his three daughters: frightened for Doreen's well-being, despite the medical staff's assurances that she was doing well, and slowly coming to terms with having five of them living in a little two-bedroom house. On top of that he was also experiencing waves of pride at becoming a father, a very old father who would be eighty before his daughters left school.

Reg and Mary stopped off at Harry's for a short while. Mary led the conversation, talking about how he was to manage over the coming weeks when the triplets came home. Doreen would need domestic help if he was to come to work, and before they left, Harry had concluded that he also needed to look for somewhere bigger than his current house.

Reg was not sure of his own feelings either, as he and Mary eventually walked home.

"Reg... you know we haven't set a wedding date. Have you any idea when we will be able to afford it?"

Reg gulped. What with Doreen giving birth, and Tracey announcing her pregnancy, he was wondering if Mary was about to tell him something he might not want to hear."

"Well, if we move into rented accommodation we could make it quite soon. But otherwise it will be a while before we have enough for a deposit on a house, and we've not seen anything we both really like yet."

"What about Tracey's house?"

"You're joking! How could we afford something like that?"

"I was talking to Tracey. The way things are going, the company will have money to invest, and she is thinking about buying property. She wondered if we would like the house two doors up from her, at a nominal rent, until we had enough to buy something of our own."

Reg was stunned. It was so far beyond his expectations that he had difficulty even envisaging it. As he did not reply, Mary waited a few moments and then continued.

"Mind you, I'm not sure how you'd like noisy neighbours. Perhaps we should look for something else."

"Noisy neighbours? How do you know the neighbours will be noisy? None of the other houses are even occupied yet."

"Oh. Didn't I tell you? Tracey's planning to persuade Harry and Doreen to buy the house next to them. She's already put down a deposit in their name on it. Three babies can make quite a racket."

Suddenly Reg began to laugh. It was in Tracey's nature to manipulate the lives of those around her, and somehow all seemed to benefit from her actions. He stopped laughing as a vision of baby-sitting, and nappy changing, crept into his mind. Mary must have had the same vision, but her reaction was to chuckle, and snuggle closer to her man as they walked.

27. LIFE – PECKHAM STYLE

Despite the upheaval in the domestic lives of some of the staff, Peckham Paints went from success to success. The phenomenon of red painted car roofs spread, but with different colours for different districts. This particular application of the paint became so common that Tracey set up a separate business, offering professionally applied paint, in a unit on a new trading estate off Dunton Road.

With great reluctance, Potter released Malcolm to run the business, for Potter had high hopes of the man as a deputy for himself on the production line. Malcolm, who had recently taken to spending his weekends camping on the Lincolnshire coast, and looked rather tired these days, was delighted.

Tracey gave him a free hand to recruit staff, and borrow men from the production line as he found necessary during the initial development of the business. Malcolm surprised everyone in his industrious and innovative approach to the work. He canvassed the local Inner London Education Authority Adult Institutes, particularly those that held art classes, for painters, and soon expanded the work to include murals as well as simple mock vinyl roofs.

A favourite scene, particularly amongst customers who saw his advert in *Hare and Hounds*, was of a full hunt in pursuit of the fox. This was often painted along the side of an old Land Rover, with the lead hounds on the rear bumper and the fox's brush showing out of the exhaust pipe. Malcolm's staff of mainly beret-wearing, old-age pensioners were delighted to create such works, and often took liberties with the faces of the huntsmen, depicting pop stars, politicians and local celebrities astride the galloping steeds. Malcolm declined to give advice to such customers regarding registering a change of vehicle colour with the DVLA.

Shortly after opening the premises, Malcolm employed a female clerical assistant to manage the administration side of the work. She was a slim brunette of about forty. As Malcolm prepared cars and painted them in the workshop, he could hear the regular chinking sound as her gold bangle tapped the metal desk whilst she typed. Malcolm viewed each day's schedule of jobs carefully every morning, and left painting red roofs until the last of his work. It was inconvenient when the woman lost her voice too early in the day, although subsequent evenings did have their compensations.

At the factory, Pat O'Keefe urgently sought out his boss, and his brother, and shepherded them into Darren's booth on the loading bay. He carefully closed the door behind them before speaking.

"I think we may have a problem," said a worried Pat.

Darren and Billy waited for the worried man to elaborate.

"You know that Harry has taken on a temporary assistant, now that Doreen is off work."

"Dat's right," said Billy, "her name's Christine."

"You knew? And you never thought to mention it to us. It's the girl from the Rivoli dance hall!"

"Dat's right. So it is, to be sure. Of course I knew. Sure, and wasn't it me self who got her der job in the first place!" Billy said proudly.

"She was not happy working at der gasworks. Not after dat night at the dancing."

Darren and Pat stared at Billy, both speechless, but eventually Pat regained his voice.

"What do you mean, you got her the job? How on earth did that happen?"

"Well now, after we left the dancing, I got to thinking. The poor girl had no one to see her safely to her home. Not after Mr Crewcut was taken away in der ambulance. So I…"

"Wait a minute, what ambulance?" interrupted Darren.

"Der ambulance dat came, and took him to the hospital."

"How did you know he was taken to hospital?"

Billy laughed.

"Where else would the ambulance be taking him to?"

"No. I mean how do you know an ambulance came to take him to hospital?"

"Well, I was worried about der poor girl, so I went back and tucked me self in the doorway of the dentist opposite. I saw Mr Crewcut being taken away together with dat fellow dat Moira laid out with der chair, so I waited until she came out. She was on her own, so I went and introduced me self, proper like, and offered to walk her home. She lives by der park."

"And she was happy for you to see her home after you had flattened her boyfriend?"

"Begorrah yes. He was not a real boyfriend, at all, at all. Just someone at work who had pestered her for a date. Dat's why she wanted a new job. I knew Mr Darren here had all the staff he could handle, what with taking on Lisa and Moira when you asked, so I saw Mr Reg in the stores, and he suggested that Mr Derry upstairs might need some help."

Billy beamed as he told his story, but Pat, who had been putting the pieces together in his mind, held up his hand to interrupt him.

"Wait a minute. If she lives by the park, why were you so late getting home that night?"

Billy, whose natural colour was a bright pink, blushed deep red: a red to match the most popular of their paint shades.

"We sat in the park and talked for a bit, until a policeman asked us if we had homes to go to. Dat was funny, of course we had homes, and I told him so too. He got a bit upset at dat, but he seemed to recognise Christine, so he calmed down.

Hers was closest, so we went dere, and did some more of the talking, and she made us cocoa with some fruitcake. We did not notice the time. Not until her mother came down and asked us. Fancy coming all the way downstairs to ask us the time. She must have had a clock upstairs, but perhaps she had left her spectacles in the parlour."

Pat stared at his brother as he spoke. Billy had not said a word to him about any of this in the fortnight since their night out.

"So that's who you've been seeing almost every night last week, when you said you were too busy to come with us?"

Billy looked shocked, and then he laughed.

"Glory be, no. We're just friends."

Pat breathed a sigh.

"No, it's her sister Angela I've been stepping out with. I'm seeing her tonight, but I won't be seeing her next week; she'll be on the late turn."

Pat raised his eyebrows at this last statement.

"Didn't I tell you? Sure to be, she's a policewoman."

Darren, who had stood, mouth agape, as Billy unfolded his story, suddenly had a very concise summary in his mind. Billy, who was probably wanted for grievous bodily harm, was going out with the policewoman sister of the star witness to the incident. He shook his head in disbelief as he watched Pat also struggle for words.

A few days later, PC Walker, whom Darren recognised as a friend of Reg in the stores, came the back way into the loading bay, and asked if William O'Keefe was there. Darren was tempted to say he wasn't, but knew that if he did so, then Billy was likely to walk onto the bay as he spoke.

"I'll go and see if I can find him."

Darren quickly found Billy, and told him of their visitor. Billy's reaction was one of mild curiosity, rather than panic at being sought by the police. He ambled out onto the loading dock, and smiled at the uniformed officer.

"Hello, again Mr Walker, Sir."

Walker nodded at Billy.

"Angela's just called me on the radio. She finished at court earlier than expected. If you're free at lunchtime, can you meet her in Jones & Higgins?"

"Dat I can, Mr Walker, Sir."

"She said for you to ask Christine to join her as well. She wants to sort out the alterations to Christine's bridesmaid dress, as well as help you choose your suit."

Darren gulped, and rushed off in a panic to find Pat.

By the time Darren found Pat, Billy had left for lunch. He related PC Walker's words, and stood with a perplexed Pat mulling over the various possible implications.

"He's known her less than three weeks. Surely you can't mean that he's proposed and she's accepted?"

"Don't know! Whatever they are planning involves a wedding, Billy getting a new suit to attend it, and Christine being a bridesmaid."

"But he bought a new suit for last Christmas. I doubt he has worn it half a dozen times since. He wore it to go to the Rivoli with us. Besides, surely he would have told me about something like that?"

Darren thought hard. Yes, Billy had been in a perfectly respectable dark blue Italian cut suit with narrow trousers and lapels, and three buttons. Almost certainly a Burton or John Collier product.

Billy returned from lunch with a large flat cardboard box, which he carefully put on an empty shelf, well away from the tins of paint. Pat picked up a few dispatch notes, and took them over to his brother.

"Hello Billy, we missed you at lunch. Been shopping?"

"Dat I have, Pat. I met Angela and Christine."

"That's nice, buy anything interesting?"

"Just bought a suit for der wedding, and a new tie. Angela gets a discount der."

"What wedding, Billy?"

"Der wedding on Saturday week."

"Whose wedding, Billy?"

"Angela's cousin. It'll be a grand do, with the reception in Park Lane. Dats up in London."

"Yes, I know where Park Lane is. Why did you need a new suit for someone else's wedding."

"I tore the sleeve of my suit when I hit dat man with the big mouth outside the Rivoli."

"What man with the big mouth?"

"Der one dat came out while I was talking to Christine, and started to shout at us. You must remember him. He was standing by the front door when we went in. Standing der in a red jacket, wid the velvet collar."

Pat thought for a moment. Yes he did remember the hall manager standing there in a maroon dinner jacket, and matching bow tie.

"You never said anything about this before, Billy. What happened after you hit him?"

"Nothing, at all, to be sure. He went over to the police van and complained. But the policeman who was driving said he saw der man being... abusive."

Billy struggled with the last word, and beamed at Pat as he proudly said it.

"What police van?"

"Der one dat Angela came in. You must remember dat! Begorrah, we heard dem coming before we left the hall."

Pat studied Billy's face, and wondered what else he hadn't bothered to tell him about that evening.

"But if the police turned up, and the manager complained to them, then how come they did not take you to the police station?"

Billy looked puzzled, as if Pat was jumping to the most unlikely conclusion.

"Why should day take us to der police station? All we were doing was standing, and doing der talking."

"Not earlier in the evening you weren't."

"Oh, dat was all sorted. Angela recognised Mr Crewcut. He must play the music, because she said she knew of his record. The police van gave Christine and me self a lift back to Peckham, but we stopped at der kebab shop, so Christine and me self walked through the park. It was Christine who suggested we sat for a while to eat."

Pat shook his head. Billy was one of life's innocents, totally unaware of the implications of events that happened around him.

"That's a relief," said Pat in a light-hearted tone, "When Darren told me that you were getting a new suit for a wedding, I thought you might be getting married."

Billy shook his head, and looked at Pat as if the man was mad.

"Dat would be silly, Pat. Angela and me self only got engaged yesterday."

28. LOOSE ENDS

Peckham Paints went from strength to strength, and under Tracey Dillon's management continued to be a very happy place to work. The annual weekend Christmas do became an eagerly awaited tradition, and it would be nice to be able to say that everybody lived happily ever after. In general they did, but there were still a few mishaps and sadnesses before that happy state arrived for most.

Sharon and Christos, after fifteen very profitable years at *The Star in The East* without a break, took a well-deserved holiday. They chose India, with the intention of having a Hindu second marriage in the shadow of the Taj Mahal. Ironically, both contracted food poisoning, and died on their fourth day of their holiday.

The doctor who examined them said that they seemed to have no defences at all against meat-carried bacteria: a consequence of many years of vegetarianism and consumption of industrial alcohol. They had a double funeral pyre in the garden of their hotel. It generated so much smoke that it caused a fatal multi-car accident on a nearby motorway.

Alfred Potter eventually learnt that his wife was co-habiting with Malcolm. Malcolm feared for his life when he heard the news, but in fact Potter was eager to speak to his wife in order to organise a divorce, and bore Malcolm no malice at all. It took several visits to Malcolm's home before Potter and she discussed the legal necessities, and it was only when Malcolm parked his red roofed car out of sight of the lounge windows that she retained her voice long enough for meaningful discussions to take place.

Potter married Edith shortly after the divorce, and together they now breed genetically modified rabbits as a hobby. The animals are very popular pets, with their pink, green and purple fur coats being most in demand, but the couple can supply a complete range of 48 different, luridly named, colours. A television interview about the rabbits, organised by the *Blue Peter* programme, was hastily rescheduled for 2am when the cameramen inadvertently focused on the colour chart, and zoomed in to pan across the individual colour names.

Harry Derry and Doreen did buy the house next to Tracey, and Christine became a permanent assistant to Harry at work, although Harry retired two years later. One of the other bridesmaids at the wedding that Angela and Billy attended eventually became a live-in nursery maid for Doreen, but that's another story altogether.

As well as the house in Honor Oak, the Derrys also have a bungalow in Dungeness: which started life as two railway carriages. Two of their daughters now drive steam trains on the Romney, Hythe & Dymchurch Railway, and the third has a very profitable house decorating business in Dymchurch. She specialises in using Peckham Paints to renovate the felt roofed bungalows that front the shingle shoreline from Dungeness to Littlestone, painting somewhat Rubenesque scenes on their seaward facing slopes. She has been accused of causing several accidents at sea, when ships pilots' spend time admiring her work through binoculars, instead of concentrating on other shipping: but nothing has ever been proved in court.

Tracey's baby was born without complication, a healthy nine-pound-six boy. He grew up to help his mother make Peckham Paints an international brand, and presently manages their Belgian manufacturing plant. The company is currently developing a bulletproof paint for the London Borough of Hackney Housing Department.

Darren left Peckham Paints to start a dance school. It was moderately successful, but closed after ten years. He and his wife, Moira, were last heard of working the cruise ships in the Mediterranean. They have six children, and whenever Moira was confined, her sister, Lisa, stepped in and partnered Darren in the ship's ballroom. Lisa had two children of her own, but will not tell anyone who the father is.

Billy O'Keefe and Angela had a long engagement, during which she encouraged him to attend night classes in English Language and English Literature, before doing an Open University degree in Literature and Journalism. Their marriage was a grand social event in the Kentish village of Whitedown where they now reside. Billy currently writes the educational supplement for a well-known Sunday newspaper, as well as plays and novels set around his rural birthplace in Ireland. His latest play, '*Potatoes and Other Friends*' has been banned in the European Union as he failed to apply for a GM Science licence before writing it.

When their two girls were old enough to be left on their own, Jane Fothergill took a job working in a new business set up by Tracey Dillon. She became chief designer at the underwear department of Kinky Klothes, a mail-order specialist garment manufacturer. She and Henry test all her new products rigorously.

Pat O'Keefe has now been engaged to Christine for seventeen years, and the couple plan to get married as soon as they can agree on the guest list for the wedding. To date they have used up forty-two reams of paper in their drafts of the list, and still have agreed less than 60% of the names as of the last draft. The average length of the list is twenty-eight names.

Recently their two eldest children have attempted to add their own input to the list, bringing the agreed percentage down from the peak of 74% agreed names that Pat and Christine achieved a few years ago.

Reginald (Piggy) Swinton and Mary Fluke did move to the house next to Doreen and Harry, but could not stand the noise from their neighbours that penetrated the thin dividing walls. They eventually moved to Devon, where they run a guesthouse at Longcombe Cross, in what is now called the 'English Riviera'. They have a number of regular guests from the Peckham area, many of them police officers.

They did not get married, as Mary was reluctant to contact her mother to get her birth certificate. Neither Reg nor Mary's mothers know where the pair are, and they plan to keep it that way. Mary tried to give up her West Country accent once they were settled at Longcombe, but the reinforcement that came with every conversation locally made it impossible. Recently Reg has caught himself using words he does not even know the meaning of. It seems to go down well with casual visitors, as does Mary's authentic Devon cooking.

James Court

THE END

ABOUT JAMES COURT

The author of the Peckham Novels was brought up in Hove, Sussex, on the slopes of the South Downs overlooking the English Channel. His grandfather worked in agriculture, and as a child he spent many a happy summer in rural Huntingdonshire, stacking sheaves of wheat and barley alongside his relatives.

After a working life spent mostly in London, he retired to the rural North Downs fourteen years ago, where he again found more time to indulge in his passion for books. For the first time since his youth he also now has time to write items longer than short stories and technical journals.

James writes humorous novels, and 'Paint the Town Red' is the final book in the series set in Peckham, south London, the other two being 'Strudwick's Successor' and 'Mulligan's Revenge'.

He also writes about rural life, especially about the 1700s, and his collection of short stories, 'Nights of Old' will be published shortly.

His rural novel, 'The Whitedown Chronicles', which is set in post-war Kent, has been published. Its sequel is currently under final revision.

More information is available on Facebook at "The Peckham Novels" or "The Whitedown Chronicles" where links to purchase e-book and paperback copies can be found.

April 2016

Printed in Great Britain
by Amazon